PRODUCT-LED ONBOARDING:

How to Turn Users Into Lifelong Customers

ProductLed Press

Praise for Product-Led Onboarding

"For most SaaS companies, the real growth problem starts when people sign up and don't stick around. This is usually an onboarding problem, and it's often the biggest weakness for most businesses. *Product-Led Onboarding* is a must-read for anyone embarking on the critical activity of improving their user onboarding."

— **SEAN ELLIS**, Founder of GrowthHackers.com and Author of Hacking Growth

"Before you can get users *HOOKED* on your product, you have to first ensure they start using it. *Product-Led Onboarding* provides a detailed, practical, how-to guide to crafting the perfect onboarding experience."

— **NIR EYAL**, bestselling author of *Hooked* and *Indistractable*

"There are countless resources out there that teach the fundamentals and best practices of user onboarding. Where *Product-Led Onboarding* really shines is its attention to the operational aspect of making those changes: how to get buy-in, how to form your team, how to run an onboarding optimization project successfully. It's a tactical primer for those who care about improving their product's onboarding experience and now need to get their organization moving in the right direction."

— **CLAIRE SUELLENTROP**, SaaS Growth Advisor and former Head of Marketing at Calendly

"Your product's growth depends on how successful you are in onboarding new users. This book offers a specific, detailed, and useful approach to improving your product's onboarding. It should be on every product and marketing leader's reading list."

— **HITEN SHAH**, Co-Founder of FYI, Crazy Egg, and KISSmetrics

---

"Our Growth Team at Wistia spent a ton of time working on new user onboarding. We knew how important it was to our success, and we had a hunch that our approach could be more effective. We had a lot of passion, but in retrospect - we had no real plan or framework to guide our thinking. This is the book I wish our team had. *Product-Led Onboarding* breaks down everything a product-led business needs to know about onboarding — from understanding your users, defining success criteria, driving engagement, and optimizing along the way. It's full of actionable takeaways that you can apply today for a big impact."

— **ANDREW CAPLAND**, Head of Growth at Postscript and former Head of Growth at Wistia

---

"If you aren't investing in your user onboarding now, it will catch up to you later. Ramli can help you nail that down! In this book, he shares an actionable, step-by-step EUREKA framework for onboarding new users — based on years of experience in the field. A must-read for product managers, marketers, and designers."

— **JANE PORTMAN**, Cofounder and CEO at Userlist

"When Ramli John and Wes Bush write a book about user onboarding, you read it. They're not only two of the most thoughtful and intelligent people I know, they're also two of the most passionate and experienced user onboarding practitioners in the world. This will undoubtedly become a go-to handbook for building great onboarding experiences."

— **ERIC KEATING**, VP Marketing at Appcues

"For anyone working in SaaS, this book is a must-read. User onboarding is likely the single most important tactic that will drive sustainable and rapid growth... yet it's also often the most overlooked. Not only does this book give you a step-by-step guide on how to build a proper onboarding strategy, but it also articulates the how. Having worked on onboarding at Hotjar, Sprout Social, and now Teamwork, I appreciate the level of detail and accountability Ramli laid out for the entire organization. From marketing, sales, product, growth, success, etc., we all play a critical part in understanding the customer journey and guiding our users to value. With this book, our teams now have a playbook that can be easily followed and absolutely nails every step in the process (in an easily digestible way). I can't wait to buy this book for my entire organization and couldn't recommend it more!"

— **TARA ROBERTSON**, CMO at Teamwork

"User onboarding is the crux to success for every business. If you can't successfully onboard users into your product to become long-term, profitable customers, your business is destined to fail. I love how the book breaks it down to an actionable framework that you can follow step-by-step."

— **COREY HAINES**, Founder of Swipe Files and former Head of Growth at Baremetrics

"Why do so many user onboarding experiences suck? Because teams try to showcase ALL THE THINGS their product can do rather than shaping it around what actually matters to customers: getting their specific jobs done. To design an onboarding experience that turns new users into happy customers, you must deeply understand your users' goals. Yet that's easier said than done. This book gives product teams a step-by-step process to follow so that they can avoid the missteps and create an onboarding experience that wow users from day one."

— **KATELYN BOURGOIN**, CEO at Customer Camp

"Retention is the foundation of sustainable growth, and it starts the moment someone perceives value in your product. This book provides you with a framework to optimize and build on that moment to raise the odds of people making your product an integral part of how they achieve their goals."

— **ANUJ ADHIYA**, Author of *Growth Hacking for Dummies*, Growth Mentor at First Round Fast Track, and VP Growth at Sophya

"Having worked with several product-led SaaS companies, a pattern I see is that poor user onboarding experience is hard to come back from and is the fastest way to lose a customer. Thankfully, Ramli John provides a powerful and practical blueprint for improving the onboarding experience."

— **ANNA TALERICO**, Operating Partner at Arthur Ventures

"This book is for everyone who wants to remain in a leadership role at their tech company. PLG is affecting every role from sales and marketing to customer success and engineering. PLG is the new Go-to-Market strategy and the old rules do not apply. Onboarding is where it all converges, and Ramli's *Product-Led Onboarding* is the best way to make sense of it all -- and set yourself up for success in this new era. Highly recommend it."

— **BRENNAN McEACHRAN**, CEO and Co-Founder of Soapbox

"A must-read for any software organization. Ramli takes the daunting task of user onboarding and turns it into an actionable step-by-step guide that enables Marketing, Product and Engineering teams to work together. As a marketer, this book made me think about the elegantly designed ways in which effective marketing teams begin that onboarding process before the customer actually uses the product."

— **AMANDA NATIVIDAD**, Head of Content at ShipBob

"As any business thinks about word of mouth and referrals, one must think about the whole customer experience. Not just the numbers side, but the individual experience of each person and their motivations. What Rami has done with this book is to explain a practical and relatable framework for onboarding that drives real business value. It's clear through all aspects of the book that this isn't just one person's job, but Ramli makes it easy to include multiple team members to drive a collaborative process. Don't let all the talk about product-led fool you, this is a book about people first and how your product can relate to people, which can unlock magic for your onboarding."

— **JOSH HO**, Founder and CEO of ReferralRock

"After teaching the growth process to thousands of people from companies like PayPal, IBM, and Booking.com, a growth problem I see over and over again is poor user onboarding. By learning how to better onboard new users, you will dramatically improve your acquisition cost, user retention, and revenue growth. The techniques outlined in the book will help you do that. *Product-Led Onboarding* is directly applicable, easy to read, and filled with great examples."

— **MAJA VOJE**, Growth Consultant and Instructor at GrowthHackers.com University

"One of the most valuable things I've seen as a Customer Success leader is the impact great user onboarding can have on long-term customer success, from driving adoption to reducing the load on support while increasing retention and customer advocacy. This book is hands down one of the best road maps I've seen to successful user onboarding. Implementing the best practices and techniques in *Product-Led Onboarding* is an investment in your customers, your business, and your future!"

— **DANNY VILLAREAL**, Head of Customer Success at Jungle Scout

"I love *Product-Led Onboarding*! It's the only content on onboarding I've ever read that wasn't bone-dry boring and taught me the importance and how-to practices in such a storytelling way. Wonderful lessons, great writing, engaging stories."

— **ADRIENNE BARNES**, Founder of BestBuyerPersona.com

"Every business that cares about long-term growth needs to make improving their user onboarding one of their top priorities. This is the book that will help you get it done. It gives you a step-by-step framework to build a fully optimized onboarding flow that drives higher user activation rates and engagement."

— **ETHAN GARR**, Co-Creator of BreakoutGrowth.net and former SVP of Growth at TelTech

"Ramli is a seasoned growth practitioner, and it shows. *Product-Led Onboarding* shines with stories from his learnings and practical knowledge that makes some of the growth's biggest head-scratchers digestible and human. If you're looking to up-level your onboarding or invest in scaling your startup, this is a great read."

– **EMILY LONETTO**, Head of Growth at Voiceflow

"When it comes to user onboarding, there's so much that should be obvious but still "needs to be said." This book does a great job of nailing those. I particularly appreciated explicitly highlighting the importance of cross-department onboarding teams and why there needs to be clear ownership on onboarding from end to end."

— **RONAK GANATRA**, VP of Marketing at GraphCMS

"As a SaaS consultant and copywriter, I've seen the guts of dozens of companies — including how they onboard and retain customers. Most have a piecemeal approach because they have a piecemeal understanding. This book is the most complete, systematic, and actionable resource on the topic I've come across."

— **JOSH GAROFALO**, SaaS Consultant & Copywriter at http://swaycopy.com

"*Product-Led Onboarding* is a supremely practical and useful book. Ramli John distills the most fundamental information about improving user onboarding experiences so you can turn more of your users into lifelong customers."

— **OSMAN KOC**, Co-Founder and CEO of UserGuiding

"When it comes to SaaS Onboarding, you can find thousands of articles on the Internet. They all talk about the same strategy, same approach and tactics, meh. Ramli took a different approach by deconstructing the core of what makes a good onboarding and give valuable insights. Right after the first chapters, you'll get a pretty good idea of what to do and how to provide a best-in-class onboarding to your users. Ramli's book is gold. Don't miss it.

— **PIERRE LE POULAIN**, Growth Marketing Manager at Whereby

ISBN 978-1-7777177-0-4 (paperback)

ISBN 978-1-7777177-1-1 (ebook)

Produced by ProductLed www.productled.com

Cover design, interior design, and illustration by ProductLed

To my parents, Ramon and Lina, who sacrificed everything to get me to where I am today.

And, of course, to my wife, Joanna. You are truly God's right hand upon my life.

Contents

Foreword

by Wes Bush

The best products in the world turn you into a superhero. They give you abilities you never had before. They keep you accountable.

They raise the bar for what you thought was possible.

Yet, in every hero's journey, there's a predictable storyline.

The main character faces a challenge and has to overcome it before they can become a true superhero that saves the day.

It's predictable, and the odds of success for a hero to succeed in a movie hover around 99.9% the last time I checked.

Yet, most products only turn a small fraction of their users into superheroes who are able to wield the new abilities of the product.

In fact, 40-60% of all new users to products won't even bother to come back a second time to use the product after they sign up. And out of the remaining new users who check out the product a second time, even fewer will ever pick up the superhero-like abilities that your product could have granted them.

And this isn't because your product can't grant these users, "superhero-like abilities."

Or that the person signing up for the product doesn't want these new abilities.

In fact, this is often never the case.

Who wouldn't want to be able to be more productive, make better decisions, or even lose weight?

The problem is there's a challenge that lays ahead for every user that they must overcome.

For some, it might be motivation.

For others, it might be that complexity is their kryptonite.

While others are just so busy that they simply forget to use your product without a prompt.

Regardless of the user, each and every one has their own unique challenges they must overcome if they're ever going to acquire those "superhero-like abilities" your product grants them.

Once you pinpoint this challenge and help your users overcome it, they level up in a big way.

If your product is a to-do list, your user is now much more productive.

If your product is an email marketing tool, your user can now build a personal relationship with thousands of contacts.

Or if your product is a fitness application, your user can now have more energy throughout the day.

Regardless of the product, the end goal is to help your users level up.

In this book, we're excited to show you how.

Introduction

Think back to the last time you discovered a software product when that incredible realization washed over you: life is never going to be the same again.

It felt like you just gained an exciting new superpower. Tasks that were once hard or tedious are now easier, cheaper, faster... better.

For me, this happened when I discovered Calendly for the first time, an app for scheduling meetings.

Gone were the days of checking my calendar multiple times to figure out when I'm available.

No more having to go back and forth with colleagues, clients, or podcast guests through email to decide on the best time for an appointment.

No longer did I need to send three different availabilities or adjust my schedule to fit various time zones.

It's... magic.

When this struggle-to-superpower experience is seamless, it's easy to feel an incredible sense of enchantment. When magic happens, it's hard to revert to the way tasks used to get done. The relationship created with that product is set for life. When another comes along with newer, flashier, and sexier features, it's not even an option.

The Cost of Neglecting User Onboarding

Unfortunately for most software products, this experience is anything but seamless. The signup and onboarding flow for new users are often afterthoughts to the "core" features of the software. The product team is preoccupied with releasing new features, while the marketing and sales teams are consumed with acquiring more customers.

Everyone is busy, so most new users fall through the cracks; for most software products, 40% to 60% of users will sign up once and never come back.[1]

When a product's onboarding is neglected, it's like throwing a massive party with balloons, fireworks, and a bouncy castle in your backyard, yet no one can get past the front door. It's a waste of time and resources for everyone involved:

- The product team may have spent days and hours planning and building the most exciting party in town.
- The marketing team may have spent ad dollars to promote it.
- The sales team may have focused their time and energy on providing a customized party experience to everyone invited.

The irony in all of this is that the user onboarding is usually the only aspect of a product that every single user will experience, including those who decide it isn't right for them.

So, the million-dollar question is: are you wasting the investment in the marketing, sales, and product teams with an experience that neglects the needs of first-time users? Or are you honoring that investment with a seamless first product experience?

You can't afford to neglect your user onboarding experience; your product's success depends on it. Get it right, and new users will quickly experience the value of a product. In the end, they experience a "Eureka!" moment and embrace the product into their lives and become raving fans.

On the other hand, if you get onboarding wrong, it'll have a snowball effect on growth, including user retention, revenue growth, and customer acquisition cost.

The EUREKA Framework

At ProductLed, we've worked with hundreds of product-led companies like Mixpanel, Ubisoft, Outsystems, and more to improve their user onboarding experience. As a result, we've developed a simple but effective framework that delivers an exceptional first impression. It ensures every new user experiences the true value of your product, shaping them to be happy customers for years to come.

The backbone of this book is the six-step EUREKA framework. It draws on fields of growth marketing, UX design, customer psychology, and copywriting for a step-by-step approach to improve your own user onboarding experience. Included are real-life examples of how this framework has been applied to fast-growing companies. The strategies covered are relevant to anyone working to improve their user onboarding experience. It encompasses:

1. Building a cross-functional onboarding team.
2. Identifying your onboarding success criteria.
3. Minimizing the time it takes for users to experience the value of a product.
4. Simplifying the signup process and designing the first product experience for new users.
5. Creating behavior-based onboarding emails, in-app messages, and additional communication methods.
6. Involving sales and high-touch support in the onboarding process.

Whether you're creating a new onboarding flow or improving an existing one, my goal is for you to absorb and apply the strategies outlined in this book. In doing so, new users will thrive with your product. They won't just experience the EUREKA moment with you—they'll become lifelong customers and champions for your product.

Let's get started!

Ramli John

P.S. If you have any questions or want to share how you're going to implement the EUREKA framework to your product-led onboarding, send me an email at ramli@productled.com or message me on Twitter (@RamliJohn), LinkedIn (https://linkedin.com/in/ramlijohn), or the PLG Slack Community (https://productled.com/slack). I'd love to hear from you!

Who Is This Book For

Most of the concepts and frameworks discussed in this book would be more applicable to those looking to improve an existing user onboarding experience. In several parts of this book, I assume that you have product and user data.

If you are working on building a user onboarding experience from scratch, most of the concepts in this book still apply. For now, you can skip over the parts where I ask you to review the product and user data.

How To Use This Book

At the end of each chapter, you'll find a few bulleted takeaways. Review them, jot them down in your notebook and share them with your colleagues. This book is best read as a team so you can talk about and implement the concepts.

If you're looking to improve your product's user onboarding experience, I've also included an **Action Items to Improve Your Onboarding** section to help guide you through the next steps.

How This Book is Organized

This book has three main parts:

Part I (Chapters 1 to 3): I cover the fundamentals of user onboarding; the first step to improve user onboarding is to understand what it is and why it's so important to your company's growth.

Part II (Chapters 4 to 9): I expand on each of the six steps in the EUREKA framework:

1. Establish your onboarding team.
2. Understand your users' desired outcomes.
3. Refine your onboarding success milestones.
4. Evaluate your onboarding path.
5. Keep new users engaged.
6. Apply the changes and repeat.

Part III (Chapters 10 to 11): I share the next steps, including how to involve the sales team in the user onboarding process.

Part I.
The Onboarding Fundamentals

CHAPTER 1:

User Onboarding – Your Product's First Impression

Two things remain irretrievable: time and first impressions.
— Cynthia Ozick

'd like to start by asking a simple question.

Why did you decide to read this book?

Were you intrigued by the title? Did the fancy graphic on the cover spark your curiosity? Or maybe you read or heard a summary somewhere and the topic fascinated you. Perhaps it was recommended to you by a friend or colleague... in that case, thank them for me, will you? :)

My point is in the short time you stumbled across this book, it was enough to compel you to start reading it. Those first few moments were crucial in shaping your perception of it.

This concept folds into everything – job interviews, coffee dates. And yes, even product experiences. When a user has a bad first experience with a product, chances are they'll toss it away within minutes. Even worse, they might become vocal critics stifling the growth of your company.

This is what Moz experienced when they released the first version of Moz Analytics:

> *People judge by first impressions... Many who tried [Moz Analytics] came away unimpressed. The "word on the street" (or, in our case, the web forums, conference halls, and social media discussions) said Moz had a crappy new product that wasn't worth the money. That reputation dogged us for three, long, growth-stunted years.[2]*
>
> - Rand Fishkin, founder and former CEO of Moz

It boils down to this: a product's growth depends on a users' first experience.

This is especially true for software businesses like Moz, where first impressions are formed during what we call the "user onboarding" experience.

You might be thinking, "Doesn't user onboarding start *after* a user signs up for a product? Isn't the first impression formed *before* the user onboarding?"

That's the problem with this term. It's vague and has varying definitions – even to people in the same company. How are you supposed to have great user onboarding if your team isn't on the same page about it?

Three Common Myths About User Onboarding

Some define user onboarding as teaching users how to use a product. Others call it a quick tour, with a few emails highlighting key features. Many believe it shouldn't be required at all, that users should be free to explore the product themselves.

Let's first become clear about what user onboarding *isn't* by busting three common onboarding myths.

Myth #1: The goal of user onboarding is for someone to experience that first "Aha" moment.

You can't bring up user onboarding without bringing up the term "Aha" moment. It's this magical moment for new users when the clouds open, and a realization hits them like a gorgeous ray of sunshine from the heavens.

"Ah, I now understand what your product does and how it can help solve my problem." All of a sudden, everything just clicks.

The "Aha" moment is the holy grail of user onboarding… or is it?

If you think the first "Aha" moment happens after users sign up, then it usually means you've lost a lot of people already. Because the majority of users never actually make it that far.

These "Aha" moments start at the first *touchpoint*. A touchpoint is any interaction that users have with a business; whether it's seeing the link on a search results page, watching a video ad on Facebook, or reading a newsletter their colleague forwarded them. A successful first touchpoint helps people visualize a product in the context of their own situation.

Like years ago, when Dropbox first came out and you saw a video of it in action: "Wait a second, I drag my files into one folder and they're automatically on *all* my devices?"

Or seeing an ad from Netflix: "Hold on, I can watch any movie for *one flat fee* every month? Plus, I don't have to go to the video store or deal with late fees?"

Or hearing from a friend how 1password works: "So you're telling me I can have those fancy, super-secure passwords with those funny symbols for each of my logins... and I don't have to remember *any* of them?"

But user onboarding doesn't stop at the first touchpoint.

Successful users go through a series of "Aha" moments before, during, and after they sign up for a product. With each "Aha" moment, users receive increasing value from a product in a series of steps; they jump to a higher value as they perceive and experience a product's capabilities.

Here's what an "Aha" journey might look like:

- While surfing a website: "Aha! I understand how this product can help me."
- Once they've signed up: "Aha! I've tried the product out for the first time and it's useful."
- After using the product several times: "Aha! I've adopted this product into my workflow and it's saving me a ton of time."
- Finally, once they start telling others about it: "Aha! I've invited my colleagues and we're working more efficiently together."

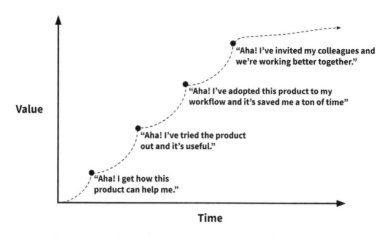

The user onboarding journey is not about driving users to a singular "Aha" moment, but instead guiding them through a series of "Aha" moments. The implication is that the user onboarding experience starts *before* users even sign up for your product, which leads to the second user onboarding myth.

Myth #2: User onboarding starts after a user signs up for a product.

When Dave McClure, founder of 500 Startups, came up with the Pirate Metrics Framework, it provided an easy way to categorize the user journey in five steps: Acquisition, Activation, Revenue, Retention, and Referral—AARRR for short (...like a pirate. Pirate metrics, get it?).[3]

In this framework, the first touchpoints with users are part of the Acquisition Step. In this step, the marketing or sales teams work to increase awareness, traffic, and sign ups for a product. It's also when users form their first impression.

Many assume that user onboarding fits into the Activation Step – when new users *interact* with a product for the first time. The goal is to guide users through to discover the value of the product.

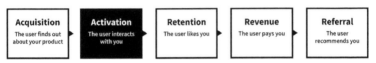

The problem with this definition is that it dismisses the Acquisition Step's critical role in user onboarding. The Acquisition Step is when a product's positioning and perceived value are communicated. If unattainable or confusing expectations are set during the Acquisition Step, good luck with successfully onboarding new users.

For instance, if the marketing and sales team overpromise features that the product can't do, it'd be almost impossible to successfully onboard new users. They'll sign up with high expectations and be disappointed when the product underdelivers from what was promised.

Another example is when there's a mismatch between what users think your product is (a.k.a. the product's positioning) versus what they experience after signing up. Let me give an extreme example. Suppose someone completely messes up the positioning and messaging of a product, so users think that the product is a project management software when it's actually a bookkeeping tool. No product tour, in-app messages, or other onboarding tactics can save this situation.

To be successful in onboarding, you need to plant the seed of future value at the very first touchpoint – whether that's in a Facebook ad, a referral from a friend, or an invite email from a colleague. With crystal clear product positioning and messaging, you can screen out people who *shouldn't* be signing up for a product early on and be able to focus more time and resources on providing incredible experiences for people who *should* be using it.

It's critical for the marketing team and (if you have one) the sales team to be involved in the effort to improve user onboarding. This ensures that everyone working on improving the onboarding experience is aligned on the positioning and messaging of the product. As I'll discuss further in Chapter 4, every great user onboarding experience starts with a cross-functional onboarding team working collaboratively to make it happen.

Going back to the Pirate Metrics Framework, we can now assess user onboarding crosses over both the Acquisition and Activation Steps. The next question is, when does user onboarding end?

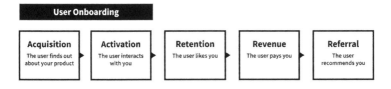

Myth #3: User onboarding ends after a user becomes a paying customer.

Another common misconception is that user onboarding ends the moment they become a paying customer. The problem with this is that users could be paying for a product *even though they're not getting any value from it.*

As Jonathan Kim, founder of Appcues, observed, paying users are not the same as successfully onboarded users:

> *Because our price point is relatively low, people would hit the end of the 14-day trial period and just buy the product, with the intention of testing it out later. Unfortunately, a lot of people apparently got distracted, didn't circle back to fully test out the product, and churned.*[4]
>
> - Jonathan Kim, Founder of Appcues

The lesson here is to be careful: don't assume a paying customer equates to a happy customer. For subscription businesses like SaaS, you know you've encountered this problem if you see a high volume of new, paying customers cancel their account soon after their first payment.

So, when does user onboarding end if it's not when users become paying customers?

To answer this, let's take a look at Slack, a channel-based messaging platform that helps teams work together more effectively.

How do you think Slack defines a successfully onboarded user or team?

You might assume it's the first time someone signs up and sends a message. Others might expect it's when ten people have joined the same Slack channel. Or perhaps it's more complicated: when 11 people have joined the same channel and sent 100 messages.

But here's how Slack defines a successfully onboarded team:

> *Based on the experience of which companies stuck with us and which didn't, after any team has exchanged 2,000 messages, 93% of those customers are still using Slack today.*[5]
> – Stewart Butterfield, CEO and Co-founder of Slack

For Slack, a team is not successfully onboarded until they've sent not one, not 10, but 2,000 messages. It's at this threshold where they've found the teams who continue using Slack going forward.

Of course, acquiring a new paying customer is fantastic. But you can't build a successful business on one-off customers; they need to keep coming back. Considering it costs up to five times more to acquire new customers than to retain them, you should work on increasing customer retention.[6] Even a small amount, say 5%, can boost profit anywhere from 25 to 95%.

For this reason, the end goal of user onboarding is not only to convert users into paying customers but to make sure they stick around for a long time. The initial user onboarding experience ends when a signal is received that the user is gaining meaningful value from a product **and** is likely to continue using it. As part of the EUREKA framework, I'll show you how to figure out an onboarding success metric in Chapter 6.

So if we go back to the Pirate Metrics Framework, user onboarding bridges the Acquisition and Activation Steps and leads into the Retention Step.

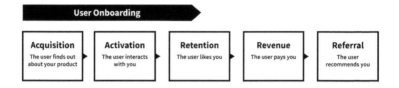

What Is User Onboarding?

Now that we have a better picture of what user onboarding is *not*, let's define what user onboarding *is*:

> User onboarding is the process that takes people from perceiving, experiencing, and adopting the product's value to improve their lives.

There are three important implications of this definition.

1. The End Goal of Onboarding

The goal of the entire onboarding experience is to help users improve their lives. It's important and helpful to view onboarding not as an exercise in teaching users about a product but rather how it makes them successful. For that reason, onboarding shouldn't be defined by how many features users have adopted. Instead, it should be determined by how much their lives have been improved.

For example, people consume Netflix not because they enjoy streaming videos. They watch it because it relaxes them after a long day at the office.

People adopt Slack not because they need another messaging tool (we already have a ton of those). It's because it helps them share knowledge, resources, and information effectively within a team, all while cutting back on email.

Samuel Hulick, a UX strategy consultant and founder of useronboard.com, uses Super Mario Bros. to visualize this concept.[2] As a kid playing Super Mario Bros., you're not excited about a fire flower because it has a green stem, and it's easy to pick up. It's because once you pick it, you become a fireball-shooting Super Mario.

In the same way, user onboarding shouldn't focus on the product (the fire flower) and its characteristics (green stem and easy to pick up)... even though they are important.

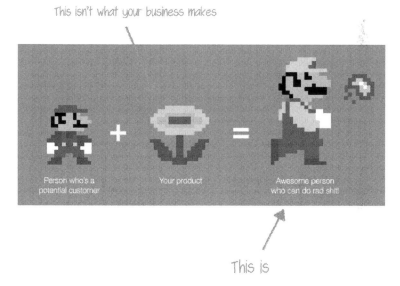

How are you helping enhance users' lives with your product? Are you helping them relax like Netflix, or communicating within teams like Slack? Whatever it is, user onboarding is a means to get there.

2.   The Three Key Onboarding Success Milestones

To successfully onboard new users to a product, they have to achieve three key milestones:

1. **The Moment of Value Perception (MVP)**: This is when users first visualize a product in the context of their situation. For the initial onboarding of new users, the MVP usually occurs before signing up.

2. **The Moment of Value Realization (MVR)**: This is when users first experience a product's value and achieve their desired outcome with the product for the first time.

3. **The Moment of Value Adoption (MVA)**: This is when users start using a product regularly and integrate it into their life or workflow.

Notice how these milestones align with the "Aha" moments mentioned earlier. That's why "Aha" moments can also be referred to as value moments. Together, these value moments form a **value path**.

Here's what Slack's value path looks like:

- **Moment of Value Perception**: Users first grasp how Slack can help their team communicate and share information more efficiently than email or other messaging tools.

- **Moment of Value Realization**: Users send their first message to a colleague using Slack.

- **Moment of Value Adoption**: Users from the same team send 2,000 messages.

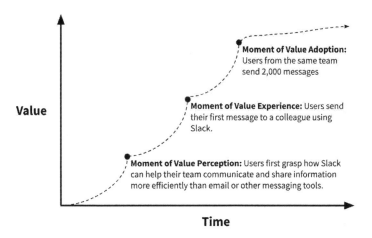

Some would argue that user onboarding is only about helping users experience the value of a product. I'd argue that this is often not enough. Experiencing the value of a product once does not mean new users will continue using it.

Think about it for a second.

Let's say you want to take up daily running in the morning every day so you can stay fit, feel healthy, and have more energy for your day. That first-morning run, you experience a runner's high–a brief, deeply relaxing state of euphoria.

But the next day, your body is in pain, and you sort of feel like a troll, dragging your body around from one place to the other. But, the more often you run, the easier it becomes. Soon, it's a habit.

The lesson here is that doing something once is not enough to build a habit. The first time you do it, you might decide that it's not for you. Or maybe it's too hard, and you don't think it's worth it. But if you do a behavior or activity enough times, it becomes easier and comes naturally without much prompting or reminder. Habits are built through repetition.

Similarly, one of the big goals of onboarding is helping users let go of the old way they performed tasks to embrace new habits with a product. Habit-forming user onboarding experiences require users to experience the value of a product more than once. Once new users have used the product enough times, they're more likely to continue using it going forward.

This is the reason why Slack defines a successfully onboarded team once they've sent 2,000 messages.

3. A Cyclical Process

The final implication is that user onboarding is a process. It involves a series of actions that uses both tools and people to provide new users the knowledge, skills, and behaviors to interact with a product effectively.

User onboarding is not a linear process. Instead, it's cyclical. Because it never actually ends.

After the initial onboarding experience for new users, they can (and should) go through a new cycle of perceiving, experiencing, and adopting additional features, capabilities, or use cases of your product. (In Chapter 9, I give tips on how to onboard new users beyond the initial onboarding.)

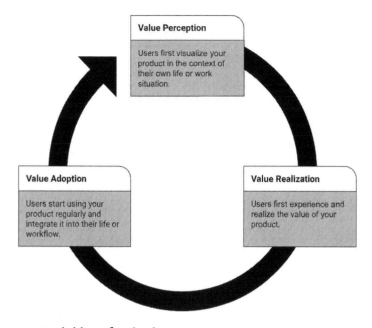

Much like a flywheel, gaining momentum to start requires considerable effort. New users have to overcome friction, such as letting go of old habits or moving past the anxiety of change. But once users complete each cycle of perceiving, experiencing, and adopting, they achieve an increasing level of value over time.

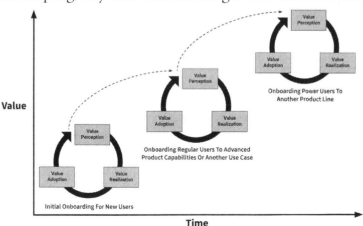

Let's look at how this is done with Intercom, a messaging platform that allows businesses to communicate with prospective and existing customers online.

Here's what a user journey could look like with them:

1. The initial onboarding cycle helps companies install live chat software on their website. This speeds up their acquisition time because they can respond to queries from prospects in real-time as visitors are surfing through pages.

2. Once users have started regularly using Intercom's live chat feature, the onboarding team helps users add smart logic that directs conversations to relevant help articles or blog posts.

3. The next level helps companies automate conversations using chatbots.

With this example, the Intercom onboarding team assists users by providing more value over time. What's even more important is that they're encouraging users to upgrade their pricing tier: from $39 to $499 per month.

As you can see, onboarding customers to additional capabilities and use cases of a product is critical for revenue expansion and increasing the average revenue per user (also known as ARPU). But first, new users need to complete the initial onboarding.

Overcoming Inertia

Like with any flywheel, getting it going requires overcoming friction and inertia. That's why the first cycle of user onboarding for new users will take the most effort and time. This is where most opportunities and low-hanging fruits lie. As we'll see in the next chapter, nailing the initial user onboarding experience is the crux of the product-led growth strategy.

Chapter 1 Summary

- Successful user onboarding experiences guide users through a series of "Aha" or value moments before, during, and after users sign up for your product.
- If you are going to be successful in onboarding new users, you need to plant the seed of future value at the first touchpoint. It's not an exercise in helping users try your product, but rather how your product can make your users successful.
- User onboarding is the process that takes people from perceiving, experiencing, and adopting the product's value to improve their lives.
- User onboarding has three main components:

i. The Moment of Value Perception (MVP) occurs when users first visualize your product in the context of their situation.

ii. The Moment of Value Realization (MVR) occurs when users first experience the value of your product.

iii. The Moment of Value Adoption (MVA) occurs when users have integrated your product into their life or workflow.

- User onboarding is a cyclical process where users experience an increase in value over time as they perceive, realize, and adopt advanced capabilities or other use cases of your product.
- The initial user onboarding ends when you have a signal that your user is getting meaningful value from your product and is likely to continue using it going forward.
- Much like a flywheel, getting momentum in the beginning will require overcoming friction such as old habits and anxiety with change.

Action Items to Improve Your User Onboarding

As we'll soon see in later chapters, improving your user onboarding is a team sport. For this chapter, have discussions with several people in your team and ask the following:

- How do you currently define "user onboarding"?
- When does user onboarding start?
- How do you currently define a successfully onboarded user?

Share with your team what you've learned from this chapter and write down their thoughts about it. Ideally, they're also reading this book with you! This will later be useful as you align your team around a common understanding of what user onboarding means for your organization.

You can also share with them a PDF version of this chapter at productled.com/eureka-chapter-1

The Crux of The Product-Led Growth Strategy

Free the child's potential, and you will transform him into the world.

— Dr. Maria Montessorri

The first few years of a child's life are crucial. They are the foundation that shapes their future health, happiness, growth, development, and learning achievement. Children need proper nourishment, care, and love to blossom into their true potential. After all, these early years prepare them to become contributing members of society.[8]

This is what Dr. Maria Montessori discovered in 1907 when she opened a school in a slum-ridden district of Rome. Montessori's "school" was just a few rooms in an apartment building intended for poor families. Her students were a group of three to six-year-old children who had never stepped foot inside a classroom before. Most expected her to fail.

Dr. Montessori got to work to implement the educational materials and methods she developed. She replaced the heavy furniture with child-sized tables and chairs light enough for the children to move. She brought in low shelves so the children could access educational materials on their own. Dr. Montessori also gave her students the freedom to choose and carry out their own activities at their own pace and following their own inclinations.

Thanks to her methods, the children started showing extraordinary understanding, activity, and confidence. By working independently, her students became autonomous and self-motivated.

News of these remarkable children began to spread. People around the world began to visit the classroom. No one could believe the children's transformation until they saw it in person. Even Queen Margherita of Italy's royal family made her way through the slums of San Lorenzo to see them!

And it all started with Dr. Montessori's belief that a child's potential can be unlocked early on with the right methods and materials in place.

Much in the same way, the earliest stages of the customer journey are crucial in setting new users up for long-term success. By treating them with intentional care during the user onboarding, you lay the groundwork for everything to come. As discussed in the previous chapter, user onboarding directly impacts the future growth of a product, and it starts during the first steps in the Pirate Metrics Framework.

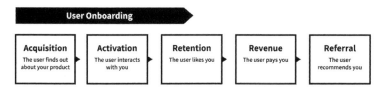

One of my goals with this chapter is to help you get buy-in from the rest of your team on how important user onboarding is to the company's growth. From my experience, CEOs and company executives realize way too late that they have an onboarding problem, so they don't invest time and resources on it.

So, in this chapter, you'll learn the three reasons why user onboarding is so important in a product-led growth (PLG) go-to-market approach and why it's often overlooked and neglected by companies. We'll also look at the five signs of bad user onboarding experiences.

If you and your team are already excited to improve your user onboarding experience, feel free to skip this chapter.

Three Reasons Why User Onboarding Is Important

As we'll soon see, the data doesn't lie – user onboarding is the crux of the product-led growth strategy. It's where it all starts.

Here's why.

1.   User onboarding is a retention lever

No matter what industry you're in, the best customers don't abandon you after their first purchase. They come back time and again for more.

Though it's an often-overlooked metric, retention plays a significant role in boosting revenue. That's because it increases the customers' lifetime value (CLV).

Retention starts with user onboarding – and the numbers prove it.

ProfitWell studied about 500 different software companies spread between business-to-business (B2B) and business-to-consumer (B2C) companies. They found that customers with a positive onboarding experience were more likely to stick around than those who weren't happy with it.

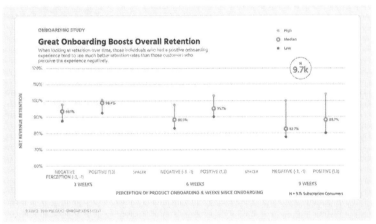

HubSpot saw this first-hand with Sidekick, an email tool for salespeople. After making positive changes to the way they nurtured new customers in Week One, they saw a 15% lift in retention during that week. This catapulted into a 50% increase in retained users after ten weeks.[2]

WEEK 1 IMPROVEMENTS

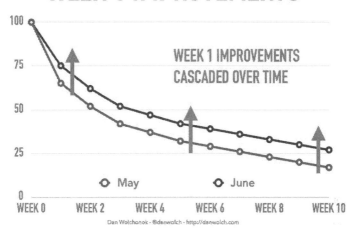

What happened at HubSpot Sidekick is not an outlier.

InnerTrends saw similar data points: users who completed the initial onboarding process were 38% more likely to return one week later.[10]

But it goes even further than that. The effects of user onboarding are even more pronounced once users hit Week 12. For those who completed InnerTrend's onboarding process, the retention rate is almost three times higher.

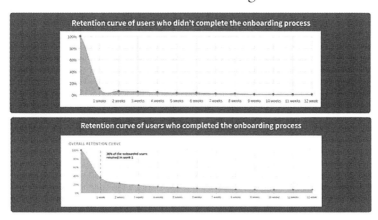

When someone first signs up for a product, they'll either love it or leave it. Those that are successfully onboarded see the value from it and are more likely to stick around, even years later.

This is especially true for SaaS companies:

In working with a number of SaaS portfolio companies, I have found that there are two causes of churn that occur more frequently than any others. They are: failure to successfully onboard the customer and loss of the champion who drove the purchase.[11]

– David Skok, General Partner at Matrix Partners

2. User onboarding is a revenue multiplier

A truly fabulous user onboarding experience converts to a revenue multiplier. This is a direct result of improving retention.

We have the numbers to prove it (get ready for some math!).

Let's go back to the example from HubSpot, where they saw a 15% increase in retention across ten weeks as a direct result of improving user onboarding.

How much did their revenue increase because of this change?

Let's say they started with 1,000 users and charged each user $5 per week without a free trial period. If you add up the revenue across all ten weeks, it adds up to $21,275. Assuming the revenue and retained users remain the same for the rest of the year at $750 each week after Week 10, the revenue totals $52,775 in 52 weeks.

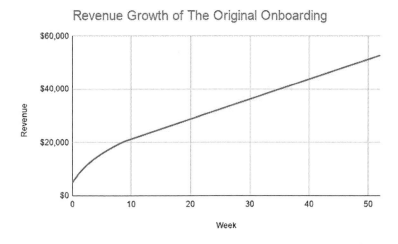

Revenue Growth of The Original Onboarding

Now let's compare that to what happened when they nurtured new customers properly with an improved experience. The revenue from Week 0 to Week 10 adds up to $26,425. Even more remarkable is if the number of retained users and revenue remain the same for the remainder of the year after Week 10. That's $78,925 in annual revenue, which is a striking 50% increase.

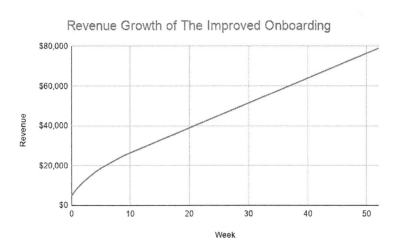

Revenue Growth of The Improved Onboarding

All thanks to a better onboarding experience!

Imagine this is for one cohort of 1,000 users.

Let's assume that they can consistently get 1,000 new users to sign up each week for the rest of the year. If we assume their new signup growth remains flat at 1,000 new customers per week for one year, the improved user onboarding experience would account for a massive increase of 49% to the monthly recurring revenue (MRR)!

So you see, small improvements in treating new customers with care can result in enormous growth.

Plus, those who have a positive onboarding experience are more willing to pay.[12]

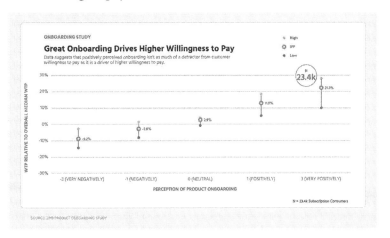

The point? User onboarding really does set the stage for future success and has a huge impact on your revenue growth.

So it comes as no surprise the biggest weakness in growth stems from that initial first impression:[13]

The real growth problems start when people land…and leave. They don't stick. This is an onboarding problem, and it's often the biggest weakness for startups.

    - Casey Winters, Chief Product Officer at Eventbrite

3. Good User Onboarding Leads To Lower Customer Acquisition Costs

If having an incredible user onboarding experience is a retention lever and revenue multiplier, bad onboarding can lead to higher Customer Acquisition Costs, CAC.

The CAC is easy enough to calculate. Divide all the costs spent on acquiring customers (a.k.a. marketing expenses) by the number of customers acquired in the time period the money was spent.

For example, let's say a company spent $100 on marketing in one year and acquired 100 customers in the same year. Their CAC is $1.

$$\frac{\$100 \text{ (marketing)}}{100 \text{ (acquired customers)}} = \$1$$

Let's revisit the previous example of Hubspot Sidekick. Let's assume it costs $2,000 to acquire 1000 new users and, in this scenario, there's a seven-day trial.

After one week, they have 600 paying customers with the original onboarding or 750 customers thanks to the new onboarding. That amounts to a CAC of $3.33 for the original onboarding and $2.67 for the improved onboarding.

A 15% increase in retention means CAC went down by 20%.

Original Onboarding	Improved Onboarding
600 new users = $3.33 CAC	750 new users = $2.67 CAC

Which one would you prefer to see in your company's own metrics?

Alright, let's put this another way.

Perhaps you spend $1 to acquire new signups, converting at 1%. That CAC is $100. But, if you optimize onboarding and increase the percentage of active users who become paying customers from 1% to 2%, that CAC cuts in half to $50.

Excellent onboarding has an abundance of payoffs: it leads to higher activation rates and, subsequently, a lower CAC.

If you're losing 60% of your new users after the first session, it doesn't make sense to spend a ton on acquiring signups or your CAC will be high. The unit economics will not work out. [14]

— Francois Bondiguel, Growth Head of B2B Marketing and Growth at Canva

The Ugly Duckling of Growth – User Onboarding

Helping new users to perceive, experience, and adopt a product's value is critical to long-term retention, revenue, and profitability. This doesn't just appear out of thin air. It takes a well-thought-out strategy to make the magic happen.

User onboarding is often treated like the ugly duckling of growth. It's largely ignored or assigned as a low priority task to the product or customer success team.

But if it's so important in a product's growth story, why don't the majority of teams invest their resources to improve it?

After working with hundreds of product-led companies, we've found a few answers to this perplexing question. The ProductLed team has identified five challenges you might face when trying to improve this experience.

Note: In the next chapter, I'll provide a framework to help you overcome these challenges.

1. No clear ownership of user onboarding

Who is responsible for the user onboarding experience? Is it the product team or the customer success team?

If no one owns it, then it won't be prioritized and falls through the cracks. As a result, it takes weeks or even months to see any boosts.

2. Only the product team works on improving user onboarding

This happens because companies believe the first two onboarding myths: that user onboarding starts after a user signs up for the product and ends when users become paying customers. To deliver a seamless onboarding experience, improving it needs to be a cross-functional effort that involves a variety of teams: stretching from sales, marketing, product, and customer success.

3. Misaligned definition of user onboarding across teams

Imagine being in a rowboat, and everyone is rowing in different directions. Good luck getting anywhere in a timely and efficient manner. This is what happens when a product team views user onboarding differently from how other teams see it. It's important to ensure each team has a clear, aligned understanding of what user onboarding is.

4. No clear quantitative criteria for successfully onboarded users

If you don't know your destination, then good luck getting there. You need a clearly defined success metric to determine if users have been successfully onboarded or not.

Now the big question is: how do you know when a user has adopted a product into their life or workflow? More on this later.

5. No clear strategy to continuously improve user onboarding

You can't just slap on a product tour, send a few onboarding emails, and believe you're going to move the needle. That's risky behavior. It would help if you had a specific strategy in place based on user research and data. Otherwise, you risk losing users with annoying product tours or spammy emails.

Furthermore, you can't just work on improving your user onboarding once a year. As you introduce new features to your product, you have to seamlessly integrate these into your onboarding without it becoming bloated.

Five Common Signs of Bad User Onboarding

If you're reading this and have had a few "Eureka!" moments of your own, then good! You're acknowledging the pitfalls within your own company. A lack of strategy and ownership are two key elements you won't want to ignore for too long. Because if you do, you risk stifling your company's growth.

Like a detective, you should always be on the lookout for signs and symptoms of bad user onboarding.

Not sure where to start?

Here are five common signs of bad user onboarding:

1. Users don't complete your signup process.

If new users jump through hoops during the signup process, you'll lose them even before they try your product.

Examine your analytics to determine if new users are getting stuck in the signup process. Are you asking them for a bunch of information that has nothing to do with their initial use of the product?

These are called non-essential fields. They typically consist of questions like, "How many employees do you have?" or, "What are your CRM systems?" Each company will have a different definition of what non-essential fields are. It's your job to determine if these questions are hindering your signup goals.

These aren't only hurting your completion rates. It's biting into the profit margin, too. Marketo found that a few non-essential fields in the signup process increased their cost per lead by up to 25%.[15]

Short Forms Outperform Long Forms

Marketo

	Short Form (5 fields)	Medium Form (7 fields)	Long Form (9 fields)
Conversion:	13.4%	12.0%	10.0%
Cost per:	$31.24	$34.94	$41.90

Sure, every field you ask users to fill out could help you learn more about them. One could also argue that with more signup fields, you'll get higher quality signups because only the most motivated users end up completing it. But, each field in a signup form *could* be losing you new users. So be sure to consider whether each question justifies the risk of loss.

2.   Users sign up and don't come back.

According to Intercom, 40% to 60% of users who sign up for a free trial use it once and never come back (this happens to be true for the majority of software products).

Mobile apps have it worst: 73% of mobile apps are used only once before they are deleted for good.[16]

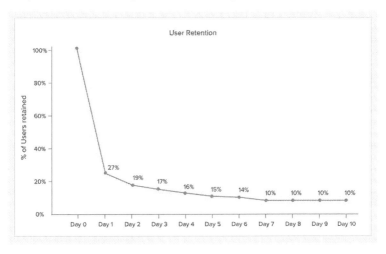

But if you deliver a stellar first product experience and help users experience the value of your product, they'll likely continue to use it.

This is critical.

It doesn't just involve product tours, either. Get creative and use external triggers like emails, browser or app notifications, and SMS text messages to convince users to return to a product.

3.   Users don't upgrade to a paid account.

Ideally, once users perceive, experience, and adopt the value of your product, they'll start paying for it. If most users don't upgrade, it could be a sign that your user onboarding needs some love.

So, what's a good free-to-paid conversion rate?

For freemium businesses, aim for a rate of 2% to 5%.[17] For sales-assisted accounts that include products with free trials, aim for a 15% trial-to-paid conversion rate. For self-serve, unassisted users, this rate will sit a bit lower, at 4%.[18]

Though, this will depend on the annual contract value (ACV) – the higher the price point, the more difficult it will likely be to convert users.

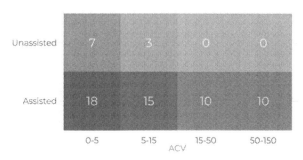

Sales Assistance Impact Evident at Every ACV
The Median Respondent with 15k-50k ACVs Converts Assisted Leads at 20%

	0-5	5-15	15-50	50-150
Unassisted	7	3	0	0
Assisted	18	15	10	10

ACV

Of course, other variables come into play here, such as the size of the industry and the stage of the company.

4.   A high volume of new customers leaves after paying their first invoice.

Have you ever continued to pay for something while not using it? Let's go back to that lovely New Year's resolution you made to hit the gym. Gym owners are very aware that some members don't stick around, so they usually require a long-term contract.

It's very rare to be forced into a long-term contract for product-led businesses. So, if users are still skeptical about the value of a product, they might pay the first invoice to extend their free trial and then cancel after that.

This is what Jonathan Kim found with Appcues when they had a 14-day trial. Because their price point was relatively low, people would hit the end of the 14-day trial period and buy the product to extend their trial.[19] Unfortunately, they found that most of these users didn't end up fully testing out their product and churned. So, the Appcues team transitioned to a usage-based free trial that expires after you show 50 Appcues product tours or tooltips on your website.

If you're finding that a high volume of new users leaves after paying their first few invoices, it could signal users are not finding enough value during the user onboarding to continue paying for it.

5.   The customer acquisition cost (CAC) is high or continues to rise.

If good user onboarding leads to lower CAC, then the opposite might imply a user onboarding problem. One reason for this could be "The Bad Onboarding Death Cycle." If you ignore user onboarding for too long, most new users won't stick around. As a result, growth flattens or dips.

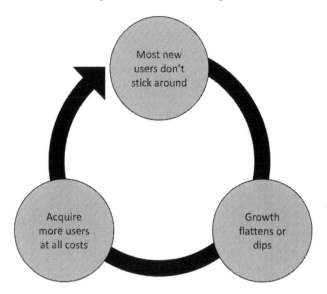

Instead of identifying and solving the root cause of the problem, teams fall into this cycle because they believe it's the easy way out. They opt to acquire more users at all costs to make up for the flattening or dipping growth rate.

This is deceiving. At first, growth starts to pick up. But since you're not investing in showing them the value, they leave. An increasing CAC is a result of this. Don't fall for the Bad Onboarding Death Cycle.

If your CAC is high or continues to rise, investigate if user onboarding has issues before continuing on.

Treat New Users With Care

Invest in those early moments with your users. By providing a stimulating learning environment, nurturing their growth and development, and treating them with care, users are more likely to find value in a product, and thus stick around and continue paying for it for years to come.

Get it wrong, and it'll open Pandora's box. A whole host of growth problems will arrive at your doorstep: poor retention rates, decreasing revenue projections, and high CAC.

This is why user onboarding is so crucial and has such an outsized snowball effect on growth – it allows users to unlock the inherent value of a product.

Chapter 2 Summary

- Three reasons why user onboarding is the crux of product-led growth strategy:

    i.   **User onboarding is a retention lever.** For example, the HubSpot Sidekick team found a 15% lift in retention during the first week of new users resulted in a 50% increase in retained users after ten weeks.

    ii. **User onboarding is a revenue multiplier.** If you started with 1,000 users and charged each user $5 per week without a free trial period, a 15% increase in the retention during the first week of new users will result in a 50% increase in revenue.

    iii. **Good user onboarding leads to lower CAC.** Assume it costs $2,000 to acquire 1000 new users and there's a seven-day free trial. Let's say improving the user onboarding improved the trial-to-paid conversion from 60% to 75%. That's a CAC of $3.33 for the original onboarding or $2.67 for the improved onboarding...

- User onboarding is vital because it sets the stage for everything to come, including retention and revenue.
- There are five challenges companies face when improving their user onboarding experience:

    i. No clear ownership.

    ii. Only the product team works on user onboarding.

    iii. Misaligned definition of user onboarding.

    iv. No clear quantitative user onboarding success metric.

    v. No clear strategy to continuously improve user onboarding.

- Five signs of bad user onboarding:

    i. Your users don't complete the signup process.

    ii. Your users sign up and don't come back.

    iii. Your users don't upgrade into a paid account.

    iv. You have a high volume of new customers leave after paying their first invoice.

    v. Your customer acquisition cost is high and continues to increase.

Action Items to Improve Your User Onboarding

In this chapter, we discussed the importance of user onboarding with sample data. As stated earlier, my goal with this chapter is to help you get buy-in from the rest of your team on how important user onboarding is to a company's growth.

Share this chapter with your team. You can download the PDF version of this chapter at <u>productled.com/eureka-chapter-2</u>.

If you know how to, create the retention curves for users who did and didn't complete your current onboarding process. If you don't know how to, I cover this in more detail in Chapter 6.

CHAPTER 3

An Overview of the EUREKA Framework

Building a good customer experience does not happen by accident. It happens by design.

— Clare Muscutt

n the first 15 seconds of every new experience, people are lazy, vain, and selfish.

It sounds harsh. But I didn't say it. Scott Belsky, Chief Product Officer at Adobe, did.[20]

It's an observation that before users feel invested in a product, they're all looking out for number one first – themselves.

Think about the last time you tried out a product. What thoughts and questions came to mind first?

- "How will this product help me?"
- "How is this product better than what I'm doing right now?"

- "How will I look if my friends or colleagues found out I'm using this product?"
- "Why would I want to drop what I'm currently doing and replace it with this?"

First, these questions show that we are lazy. We don't have the time or energy to figure out what a new product is or what it's not. We want to know now. We have no patience to read long directions. We have no time for steep learning curves. Our default is to find the easiest and quickest path to what we want.

Second, we are vain. We care about how our friends and colleagues perceive us. Once our physiological and safety needs are met, we look for ways to feel loved, connected, and accomplished by others.[21] Whether it's social apps like Instagram that help us receive more "likes" or a visual reporting tool to help us create presentations at work, products tap into our social needs.

Finally, we are selfish. Even when we're trying out a product that could help the team be more productive or protects the environment, we want to know what's in it for us. That's why assisting new users to achieve quick wins is critical, regardless of a company's long-term vision.

That's the real challenge with onboarding—people want the most value for the least amount of time. They are pressed for time, so you have a short window of opportunity to grab their attention and show them the product's value.

Time-to-Value

For this reason, one of the most impactful tactics to improve user onboarding is to minimize the time-to-value (TTV) as much as possible. This is the amount of time it takes a new customer to realize value from a product.

It's important to note here that the goal is not to have the *shortest* possible TTV, but the *minimum amount* of time for people to experience the product's value, so they continue using it going forward. This nuance is incredibly important. Some friction is actually good to successfully onboard new users. I'll discuss this more in Chapter 7.

In a sales-led business model, you can get away with a longer TTV since, in most cases, the customers paid upfront, and they're usually stuck in an annual contract. Even if it takes a considerable amount of time from purchasing the product to experiencing its value, it's typically too late for the customers to back out.

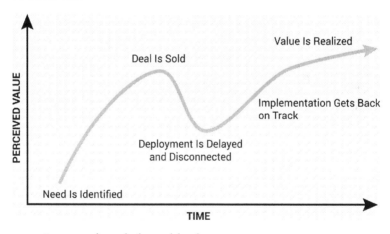

In a product-led world where users are easy-come-easy-go (because there is usually no upfront cost), the tolerance for delays and frustrations is much smaller. If your TTV is too long, new users will leave... for good.

Process over Prescription

So, how do you improve a product's user onboarding to reduce the TTV?

To make it very simple, I could give you a list of best practices and attributes of bad versus good onboarding, like below:

Bad Onboarding	Good Onboarding
• Gets in the way of users • Isn't relevant to users • Focuses on converting users too soon without letting them try the product • Overwhelms users by showing and teaching them too many things too soon • Delivers a one-size-fits-all experience for every segment served	• Complements the product • Helpful, topical, and contextual to where users are in the customer journey • Focuses on helping users experience and adopt the value of a product • Personalizes the onboarding experience based on the user's desired outcome

But adopting the wrong best practice could do more harm than good. Being too prescriptive dismisses how unique a product, market, team, and users are.

For example, some users love heavy-handed product tours, while others find it annoying. Some might feel overwhelmed with too many onboarding emails, while others might want more tips and resources.

Instead of explaining what you should and should not do with user onboarding, my goal is to provide a framework and process to help your users perceive, experience, and adopt your product.

The EUREKA Framework

Along with Wes Bush and the ProductLed team, I've worked with hundreds of organizations to improve their user onboarding experience from the very first touchpoint. Called the EUREKA framework, this six-step process will shorten the TTV for more new users to be successfully onboarded to your product:

1. **Establish your onboarding team:** To deliver an effective, immersive, and seamless onboarding experience for new users, your approach needs to be collaborative across functions and departments. Onboarding can't just be quilted together from the work of different teams. It must be holistic. If it's not, users will receive a fractured experience. In the next chapter, I'll help you form an onboarding 'A' team.

2. **Understand your user's desired outcomes:** The best way to successfully onboard new users is to figure out why they signed up in the first place. Particularly, you need to know what *value* means to users. In Chapter 5, I'll help you figure out how to do that using the Jobs-to-be-Done (JTBD) framework.

3. **Refine your onboarding success criteria:** Your team needs a clear picture of what it means to successfully onboard new users. In Chapter 6, I'll help your team identify the onboarding success metric using data. We'll also define Product Qualified Leads (PQLs).

4. **Evaluate and optimize your onboarding path:** To minimize the time it takes for new users to experience a product's value, you have to map out the user's journey to discover which steps should be delayed or eliminated. In Chapter 7, we'll do just that with Wes Bush's Bowling Alley Framework.

5. **Keep new users engaged:** To help guide new users to experience a product's value, consider using triggers both inside and outside of the product. These could include product tours, welcome messages, progress bars, onboarding emails, SMS, and in-app notifications. In Chapter 8, I'll help you determine which "Product Bumpers" and "Conversational Bumpers" to use for user onboarding using the BJ Fogg Behavior Model.

6. **Apply the changes and repeat:** User onboarding is a continuous process. In Chapter 9, I'll help you analyze the results and apply the learnings into the next iteration of your onboarding experience.

Ready to experience your own EUREKA moment?

Let's go!

Part II.
The EUREKA
Framework

Establish an Onboarding Team

> *Teamwork makes the dream work, but a vision becomes a*
> *nightmare when the leader has a big dream and a bad team.*
>
> – John Maxwell

"Bond. James Bond."

From the first time I saw a James Bond movie, I've been a big fan. One weekend, I binge-watched all 24 films, starting with the first 1962 film *Dr. No* with Sean Connery, to the most recent 2015 one starring Daniel Craig in *Spectre*.

What's fascinating about James Bond is that he's invincible. No matter how many villains, bullets, and grenades are thrown at him, he escapes every seemingly impossible situation – all without a drop of sweat on his forehead. He's a one-person killing machine taking on multiple criminals alone. It's too good to be true, isn't it?

If Bond was real, it's estimated that he would have died within seven minutes of the movie *Skyfall*. After all, a uranium depleted shell penetrated his chest. Medics and nurses who reviewed the film concluded that this, "would have turned his lungs inside out and killed him."[22]

Being a hero looks great in the movies. But in real life, it rarely works out.

The reason I bring this up is to warn you of the number one pitfall I see companies make when trying to improve their user onboarding. Instead of working across multiple functions, there is usually one person or department (typically the product team) who works in a silo from the rest of the company to do it. Much like a James Bond movie, it looks great on the surface level. But in reality, it's a recipe for disaster.

User onboarding should not be a solo effort but rather a team sport. You can't approach it as James Bond does. It's important to build a dream team like Marvel's Avengers by bringing together the "superpowers" of different departments or functions. This way, you're taking a holistic approach, which allows you to deliver an effective, immersive, and seamless onboarding experience for new users.

The Importance of a Cross-Functional Onboarding Team

Cross-functional collaboration is the key to product growth. One of the damaging effects of departmental silos is how they slow innovations that drive growth.

The ability to collaborate in networks is more important than raw individual talent. But only 25% of senior executives [we surveyed] would describe their organizations as effective at sharing knowledge across boundaries, even though nearly 80% acknowledged such coordination is crucial to growth.[23]

– Authors of McKinsey Report

Often, this is exactly what happens within companies. Marketing works on a few onboarding and product marketing emails. Product focuses on UI tweaks in the signup process and first-use workflow. The sales team touches base with users once in a while, trying to convince them they need an upgrade. Support waits until a user needs help.

Every team is contributing to the user onboarding experience, but they're all doing it in isolation.

Every great user onboarding experience starts with many hands working collaboratively to make it happen. Before auditing your current onboarding flow, redesigning the first user experience, and rewriting onboarding emails, it's imperative to establish a cross-functional onboarding team. This is the first step in the EUREKA framework.

In this chapter, we'll examine the roles and responsibilities of onboarding teams. And also, who should own it and how to get started with establishing an onboarding team.

The Roles

The process to improve user onboarding works best when it's a team effort, ideally from across different functions within a company. Each team involved in the user onboarding experience holds a piece of the puzzle and can bring a unique perspective on how to best onboard new users. Ideally, teams need to be engaged from the get-go: from Acquisition to Revenue in the Pirate Metrics Framework.

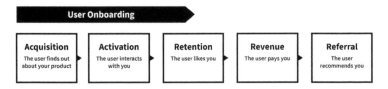

The specific makeup of an onboarding team varies from company to company and also from product to product. The size of the team will also vary widely, as does how narrow or broad-ranging the scope of their work is. At this stage, it's important to identify which teams contribute to the success of new users.

This could include the following roles:

Product Managers

Product managers typically orchestrate the in-app user onboarding experience with designers and engineers: from the signup to the first-use workflow. They oversee implementing any triggers inside your product. This includes (but is not limited to) progress bars, product tours, and checklists that help guide new users to their desired outcomes.

The role of an in-app user onboarding experience is critical because all new users are lazy, vain, and selfish in the first 15 seconds.[24] They don't have the patience to read directions, especially if the learning curve is high. They also only care about their own desires and needs. A product manager's job is to minimize the time it takes for new users to experience the value of a product as quickly as possible.

In most product-led companies, product managers are well suited to lead the onboarding team. In large part, this is because most product managers typically work cross-functionally with the marketing, user research, engineering, and UX design teams.

Marketers

Marketers communicate the value of a product. They use tools, resources, and content to educate new users to become effective, regular users. This could include crafting and managing lifecycle email campaigns, templates, case studies, and helpful tips – each designed to draw the user's attention to the core actions of a product.

Marketers are critical in the user onboarding process because no matter how good the in-app user onboarding experience is, 40% to 60% of users will sign up once and never come back.[25] By using external triggers such as onboarding emails, browser notifications, SMS messages, direct mailers, or retargeting ads (normally the job of a marketer), you can remind users how the product improves their lives.

Furthermore, great marketing builds trust and creates a personal, emotional connection. This hits every touchpoint: from ads, blog posts, and landing pages all the way to onboarding copy, in-app messages, and emails. A marketing team needs to create a cohesive and consistent content strategy that amplifies the need for a product or the pain of their situation to help them overcome their anxieties and objections.

Customer Success

Those responsible for customer success and happiness should lend a huge hand in the onboarding process. Understanding a user's wants and needs is crucial during onboarding. Customer success teams are usually equipped with the empathy and product know-how necessary to show users immediate value.

When users stumble during the user onboarding process, it's up to customer success to reach out and measure how they feel as they progress. Since they're the first point of contact for issues and problems new users face, they can provide invaluable user feedback for the business. Every support question and survey response should be recorded and relayed to where it's needed to enhance the user onboarding experience.

Sales

With hybrid or sales-assisted onboarding, it's the sales team who reaches out to potential customers to ensure they're receiving a ton of value from a product. Salespeople tend to take special care of individual users while laying out expectations for further features of the product to motivate them to build a deeper, more frequent habit with a service, such as premium features or subscription benefits.

Using product engagement data from the product and marketing teams, sales teams often use demos to provide customized walk-throughs of the product. This is how two teams can work hand-in-hand: the sales team can build on the relationships first initiated by the marketing team.

The Onboarding "A" Team

It's important here to emphasize that who should be included on the onboarding team depends on what exactly is involved in the early stages of the new user's journey. For example, someone from the marketing team may be involved in the onboarding because of the way a company's CRM tools are interconnected.

For an internal product that's used only by employees within a company, the onboarding team might just be a few product managers and a marketer. But for products sold to small and medium-sized businesses or enterprise companies, the onboarding team could consist of many teams: marketing, sales, product, design, and customer success.

Here's a summary of the roles that could be in an onboarding team.

Function	Role in Onboarding
Product	• Guides new users to high-value actions in an app. • Minimizes the time it takes for new users to experience the value of a product.
Marketing	• Communicates the value of a product by empathizing with the pain of the user's current situation. This is done from the first touchpoint to when new users have experienced and adopted the product. • Creates and sends engaging content to bring inactive new users back to the app and to move them forward into the next step of the onboarding process.
Customer Success	• Fuels product adoption by helping users find immediate value from a product. • Gathers feedback from new users and brings it to the onboarding team to improve the onboarding experience.

Sales	• Takes care of high-value users by setting expectations and building relationships with new users. (We'll explore this further in Part Three of this book.) • Offers customized and highly-targeted demos using product engagement data from the product and marketing teams.

For your onboarding, decide on who should be involved and what their primary responsibilities are. If you're wondering who should be in your onboarding team, ask yourself which team or person is responsible right now for:

- Defining your product's positioning and messaging.
- Running acquisition campaigns.
- Creating and maintaining onboarding communication such as emails, in-app messages, external notifications, or direct mail.
- Designing and implementing the user experience for the signup and first use workflows.
- Converting the free users to paying customers.
- Supporting new users if they get stuck during the user onboarding process.

Who Owns Onboarding?

This is the one question I'm always asked: who should "own" onboarding?

My response is this: it's not about *owning* but more about *championing* user onboarding within an organization. It depends on which team is the closest to the customer and has the best ability to pull in people from different departments to focus on delivering an immersive and seamless experience for new users:

- At Drift, it's the product team that champions user onboarding.
- At Jungle Scout, it's the customer success team.
- At Sprout Social, it's a cross-functional team led by marketing.
- At Facebook, it's the growth team.
- The key is that whoever owns user onboarding needs to ensure it's a cross-functional effort.

Leadership Buy-In

Due to the nature of a cross-functional onboarding team, it's important that a high-level executive is given responsibility for the team. This ensures everyone has proper authority to cross the bounds of established departmental responsibilities.

Improving user onboarding can't be a side project. It requires attention and continuous improvement—a product's growth depends on it. As discussed in Chapter 2, it's a retention lever and revenue multiplier, and works to increase profitability by reducing your CAC.

Without a clear commitment from leadership, an onboarding team will find themselves battling bureaucracy, inefficiency, and inertia. Whether it's the founder, CEO, VP of Product, or VP of Growth, someone from executive leadership needs to champion onboarding to assure sustained success.

Getting leadership buy-in is much easier said than done. Everyone doesn't just magically understand the need for an onboarding team. There is a lot of internal influence and buy-in from the highest levels of leadership, even for smaller companies.

I've created Chapter 2 with the sole purpose of explaining the benefits of improving the user onboarding experience, as well as describing the costs associated with neglecting it. You can download the PDF version of it at productled.com/eureka-chapter-2 and share it with your team.

If you want to take it a step further, create the retention curves for users who did and didn't complete your current onboarding process. I cover this in more detail in Chapter 6.

Getting The Team Started

Once you've gotten leadership buy-in and identified your onboarding team, the next step is to come to a common understanding of what onboarding means within your own company. Everyone needs to be aligned. Ask your team the same questions we discussed in the first section of this book:

- How do you define user onboarding?
- Why is user onboarding important to your product's growth?
- When does user onboarding start? Is it after a user has already signed up for your product?
- When does user onboarding end? How do you define a successfully onboarded team or user? (We'll discuss this in detail in a later chapter when I'll help you define your onboarding success metric and criteria.)
- What are the biggest opportunities and challenges in your product's onboarding?

The best way to iron out these details is to start with a kick-off meeting. Discuss the common goal of the onboarding team, who the core team members are and their functions, and why it is critical to the growth of the company. Define what success looks like and put it all in writing.

The Next Step

The next step of the EUREKA framework is understanding your user's desired outcome, where you'll gather qualitative and quantitative data about your users, such as:

- Who are your best customers? What do they do early on in the user onboarding process?
- How many new users sign up for the product and never come back? What are some reasons why?
- Why did new users sign up for your product? What triggered them to sign up?
- Where are users getting stuck and dropping off in the user onboarding journey? Why?

Before wrapping up the kick-off meeting, determine who is going to take charge to gather this data and decide when everyone is going to meet next.

Chapter 4 Summary

- User onboarding should not be a solo effort but rather a team sport.
- The specific makeup of an onboarding team varies from company to company and also from product to product. This could include the following roles:
  i. Product managers typically orchestrate the in-app user onboarding experience with designers and engineers: from the signup to the first-use workflow.

ii. Marketers communicate the value of a product. They use tools, resources, and content to educate new users to become effective, regular users.

iii. Customer success teams are usually equipped with the empathy and product know-how necessary to show users immediate value.

iv. Salespeople tend to take special care of individual users while laying out expectations for further features of the product to motivate them to build a deeper, more frequent habit with a service, such as premium features or subscription benefits.

- Due to the nature of a cross-functional onboarding team, it's important that a high-level executive is given responsibility for the team. This ensures everyone has proper authority to cross the bounds of established departmental responsibilities.

- Once you've identified your team, the next step is to come to a common understanding of what onboarding means within your own company. Everyone needs to be aligned.

- Qualitative and quantitative data should be driving the decisions for onboarding teams, not the highest-paid person's opinion.

Action Items to Improve Your User Onboarding

- Identify who should be in our company's onboarding team. You can download a fillable worksheet at productled.com/onboarding-team-worksheet.

Understand Your Users' Desired Outcomes

Make the customer the hero of your story.

- Ann Handley, Chief Content Officer at MarketingProfs

There's a saying that "hope is not a strategy."

It's actually unclear where this phrase originated, but it's been popularly exclaimed by leaders such as Barack Obama, James Cameron, Vince Lombardi, and many others.

Regardless, if you're like me, then this feels pretty intuitive. Well-planned and thought-out action is often the best strategy... not hope.

When you hope for something, it feels like unfounded wishful thinking, with no action or a plan to back it up. Any of the following sound familiar?

- "I hope my teacher gives me a better grade this semester."
- "I hope my boss won't get mad at me for coming late again."

- "I hope traffic won't be bad this morning."
- Hope is not a strategy.

But, it's such a powerful force to bring about change. Hope is a belief that your current situation can get better, no matter how big or small.

This is the reason why signing up for a new product is an expression of hope. When users sign up, they're opening themselves up to the possibility that things could be better.

Whether that hope ends in disappointment or excitement ultimately boils down to how well you understand what exactly they're hoping for. What is it about their current situation that motivated them to sign up for your product? What were they hoping to achieve with your product that they couldn't already do?

If you fail to realize this, that sense of hope can result in disappointment. You've lost a potential user. With each churned signup, your overall CAC increases. And for users, they've just wasted their time and effort trying out your product.

For this reason, it's critical your onboarding team has a crystal-clear picture of what exactly your users' desired outcomes are. This is the second step in the EUREKA framework.

If you get this step wrong, everything else will fail. Because once you're able to fully understand what users truly want, you can design a reliable onboarding flow that turns hope into excitement.

Before you think about an onboarding redesign by adding another product tour or rewriting your onboarding emails, you need to first understand your users.

A Better Life

When you boil it down, onboarding is really about changing someone's behavior so that they can experience a better life. Users are frustrated or annoyed with something, and they sign up for a product to make their lives easier.

Remember, the primary goal of user onboarding is to help users become better versions of themselves. If we go back to the Super Mario analogy, onboarding shouldn't focus on the product (the fire flower) or its characteristics (green stem and easy to pick up), even though they are important. It should focus on creating a better life.

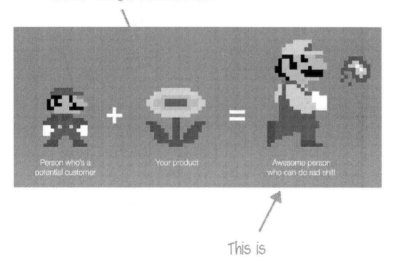

This isn't what your business makes

This is

It doesn't matter if you sell lip gloss, copywriting services, or software; people are buying a better version of themselves.

Let's say your phone is a distraction during the day, to the point work is placed on the back-burner. To combat the intrusion on your productivity, you buy a timed lockbox to keep the phone hidden. What you're *really* buying is a better way to avoid distractions from your mobile phone during work hours.

Another way to put it:

> *Upgrade your user, not your product. Don't build better cameras – build better photographers.*[26]
>
> - Kathy Sierra

Your Product's "Job Interview"

The idea of "upgrading" a user's life is at the core of the Jobs-to-be-Done (JTBD) theory by Clay Christensen, innovation expert and bestselling author of *Competing Against Luck*. JTBD is the process consumers go through whenever they aim to transform their existing life situation. To enable a life transformation, customers "hire" products to solve a problem or to satisfy a need. This is known as a *Customer Job*.

For example, a Customer Job could be: "When I'm hungry, I want to cook raw chicken so I can eat it and satisfy my hunger." So, you could "hire" a stove to make fried chicken, a grill to barbecue it, or an oven to bake it.

There are three implications of the JTBD framework.

1.   Customer Jobs are solution agnostic.

Notice how with cooking raw chicken, the Customer Job is independent of the solution (the stove, grill, or oven).

When thinking about a product's Customer Job, make sure it focuses on users' needs and problems instead of the solution. You can't start by looking at the product or what they're currently using. You have to dig to the root of the problem that caused them to start looking for a solution in the first place.

What were the circumstances around a person's life that led them to start looking for a solution?

2. The circumstances in people's lives lead to "job openings."

In the JTBD framework, understanding the circumstances and pain points in users' lives are more important than the product features and customer characteristics.

For example, after several comments from my wife that I looked like a high school student with my laptop bag, it was time for an upgrade. So, I bought a professional bag to bring to conferences and client meetings.

You could say the reason I started looking for one was to impress clients and people at conferences. But in actuality, I started to think about leveling up my wardrobe soon after I received a promotion.

While out shopping for it, a lot of information was thrown at me, ranging from the durability of the materials to the ergonomic qualities and features of the bag itself. But what actually sold me was the marketing message. This bag was made for "my grown-up work self."

So what's the point here?

To build a great user onboarding experience, it's important to know:

- What are the circumstances in users' lives that triggered them to start looking for a solution like yours?
- What is their desired outcome?

- What does success look like?
- What's holding users back from achieving their desired outcome?
- What else did they consider or try, and why didn't it work for them?

In other words, people try out products because there is a gap between their current circumstances and their final aspiration. Successful onboarding experiences are like a sturdy bridge between that gap so users can safely cross over to their desired outcome.

3. User onboarding is the Customer Job "interview."

If users are hiring a product to do a Customer Job, then the user onboarding is the "interview" process. To nail the job interview, you have to first know what job you're being interviewed to do. Do you think you'd be successful if you prepared yourself for a product management job interview if the job posting was actually for a sales development representative? I think not!

To nail the job interview with users, you must first know what job a product is being hired to do. For that, it's essential to understand the three interconnected reasons users could be signing up for a product.

The Three Components of Customer Jobs

1. Functional

When someone talks about Customer Jobs, they're usually referring to the functional component of JTBD. Functional jobs involve specific outcomes the users experience after working with a product.

Back to the example with Super Mario: the functional job of a fire flower is to make it easier for Super Mario to destroy barriers by using a new fire-spitting ability.

Another famous example is from Harvard Business School professor Theodore Levitt: "People don't want to buy a quarter-inch drill. They want a quarter-inch hole!"[27] The quarter-inch hole is the functional job the drill must do.

We can take that analogy even further by describing the purpose of the quarter-inch hole. Maybe it's to hang a photo or build a shelf. That would be the true functional job of the quarter-inch hole.

It's important to look further than what appears on the surface.

Here's another example with a SaaS business, Canva, a graphic design platform that's great for making invitations, business cards, Instagram posts, and more. At the surface level, Canva's functional job is to help people easily create custom designs. At a deeper level, it depends on *who* is using the product:

- For a paid ads marketer, Canva's functional job is to quickly create high-converting, on-brand visual assets for a social ad campaign.

- For a teacher, Canva's functional job is to create engaging visual aids that help teach abstract concepts to students.
- For a local coffee shop business owner, Canva's functional job is to create, download, and print flyers to help drive foot traffic.

Functional jobs are as complex as the number of market segments served. Segmenting and personalizing the user onboarding experience for different Customer Jobs is one of the low-hanging fruits of improving onboarding. This is exactly why Canva asks new users what they'll be using the app for during the user onboarding:

Segmentation is an important concept for the remainder of the EUREKA framework. But for now, think about the desired outcomes that users want to receive when they sign up for your product.

2. Emotional

The second component of a Customer Job is emotional: how users feel (or what they want to *avoid* feeling) after they've accomplished their desired outcome. Products meet an emotional need for people who use them, and it's a big reason why they end up purchasing.

Alan Klement, in his book *When Coffee and Kale Compete*, gives an example of this with one of Revlon's breakout magazine advertising campaigns from 1952, *Fire and Ice*. The brilliant ad campaign makes it clear that Revlon isn't selling lipstick or nail polish; it's selling a "better you." [28]

The ad barely mentions any product. Instead, it prominently features a picture of model Dorian Leigh. You need to look closely to notice lipstick and nail polish, both located near the bottom of the page.

This ad was designed on purpose to amplify the emotional component of Revlon's Customer Job.

In the factory, we make cosmetics; in the drugstore, we sell hope.

- Charles Revson, founder of Revlon

When it comes to your product, what emotions do you want your customers to feel or avoid feeling as a result of using it? For Canva users, it could be to stimulate creativity without any design training or natural visual skills.

3. Social

The third component of a Customer Job is social. When we invest time and effort into a product, we do so in a social context, whether that's at home with family or at work with colleagues. We communicate our values when we make a purchase, but we also signal to others how we want to be perceived.

Once our physiological and safety needs are met, we look for additional ways to feel loved, connected, and accomplished by others.[29]

Take, for instance, one of Canva's social ads, which reads, "No design experience? No problem. Canva makes it easy for anyone to create professional designs that are sure to get you noticed."

This ad makes Canva's social job obvious: it's to help create professional designs that your boss and co-workers will take notice of, even with zero design training or experience. You might hear them say, "Wow! This design is beautiful. I didn't know you were so creative. Good job!"

For your product, how does it impact how others perceive your customers? Are they seen as more knowledgeable? Do you make them look more professional? Do you help them become the hero in their workplace?

The Progress-Making Forces

Understanding a product's functional, emotional, and social jobs help produce a clearer picture of what your user's desired outcomes are. So how do you bridge the gap between their current circumstance to the desired outcome?

For that, you need to recognize the Four Progress-Making Forces. Pioneered by Bob Moesta and Chris Spiek of The ReWired Group, these four forces influence people to stick with the status quo or take the leap forward with a new solution:

- The **push** to find a new solution due to current problems.
- The **pull** from what could be achieved with this new product.
- The **anxiety** around the risks of moving to a new product.
- The **inertia** of not wanting to change.

The 4 Forces Influencing a Switch

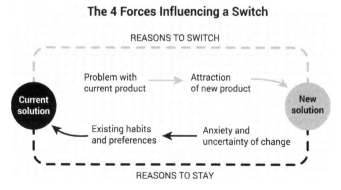

To onboard customers successfully to a complex product, you need to understand the push, strengthen the pull, calm anxiety, and overcome inertia. When we look at Canva, the reason for subscribing could involve the following forces:

- **The push to find a new solution:** "We want to experiment with different types of creatives for our Facebook ads. But we can't afford to continue hiring a freelancer to update the creatives for our Facebook ads."

- **The pull of a new solution:** "If we use a tool that provides us with templates for Facebook ads, we can get variations of creatives for our ads without having to deal with finding, hiring, and paying for a freelancer."

- **The anxiety of what could happen:** "What if Canva doesn't have any Facebook ad templates that we like? We've tried three other tools for this job, and none have been good enough."

- **The inertia of not wanting to change:** "We've already got a good working relationship with one of our freelancers. Sure, the cost and availability might be a problem. But will the designs in Canva ever be as good as a qualified designer?"

During user onboarding, Canva's team needs to amplify the pain of their current situation (the push) while at the same time explaining the benefits of the product (the pull). They need to provide guidance for complicated tasks, which helps calm anxiety while also overcoming the inertia of not wanting to change.

This approach to user onboarding helps new users deeply understand the value a product can provide while defeating the emotions that stand in the way of moving forward, no matter how complex it is.

JTBD Interviews

So how do you determine a product's functional, emotional, and social jobs, along with the four progress-making forces?

The best way to uncover valuable insights like this is through user interviews.

It might be tempting to skip this step. After all, 65% of marketing and product teams rarely do audience research.[30]

Some find executing user interviews too time-consuming. For introverts (like myself), it's a sweat-inducing experience. Whenever the ProductLed team does onboarding workshops, we have at least one person ask, "Do we really have to do user interviews?"

The answer is always, "Yes!"

Companies that invested in customer research grew two to three times faster than companies that didn't![31]

Understanding your users through customer research is the key to improving user onboarding and retention. Find the patterns in the stories of people who understand your product and understand what got them so excited to continue using it. The main focus should be to attract and create more "core users" who have fallen in love with your solution.

To do this, talk to five types of people:

1. New users - people who just signed up
2. Shoppers - people who are evaluating your product
3. Active customers - people who are regularly using your product

4. Inactive customers - people who are still paying for your product but stopped using it

5. Churned customers - people who have cancelled their account

Whether you're a seasoned pro at user interviews or just starting out, I provide a step-by-step guide to help you do user interviews in **Appendix I**. You'll get samples, templates, and strategies to summarize your research into actionable insights we've discussed in this chapter.

The useful insights from user interviews can help the onboarding team deliver a more engaged, relevant, and impactful user onboarding experience. The product team will have a better idea of which features and product actions to direct new users to. The marketing, sales, and support team can better craft messaging and prepare responses to your users' anxieties and objections.

If you get this step right, you have a higher chance of creating massive improvements in the overall onboarding experience.

On the other hand, if you get this step wrong or skip out on it, it'll trickle down to the remaining steps in the EUREKA framework. You can't help new users perceive, experience, and adopt a product's value if you don't know what value means to them. Value is not determined by a company and definitely not by the expansiveness of the feature set. Value is determined by users based on their context of use.

What's Next

When it comes to this EUREKA step, be sure to involve your onboarding team, so everyone is on the same page. Summarize your findings in the User Success Canvas we've created for ProductLed clients, which you can download for free at productled.com/user-success.

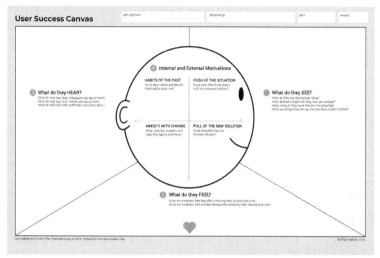

Next up in the EUREKA framework is refining your onboarding success metric. This is a tangible data point you can use to define what it means to be successfully onboarded. For example, Slack's onboarding success metric is when teams have sent 2,000 messages because they're 93% more likely to continue using it moving forward.

I'll help you identify a similar metric your team can use. It signals when new users have likely adopted your product, and the initial onboarding is complete.

Chapter 5 Summary

- The key to improving user onboarding is to gain a deep understanding of your users' current circumstances and what their desired outcome is.
- You want to know:

i.   The functional, emotional, and social jobs that your users are looking to hire a product or service for.

ii. What their desired outcome is.

iii. Any anxieties, objections, and frustrations they might have to switch from their current circumstance.

iv. Other existing solutions they're currently considering.

v.   The number one reason why they chose your product or service over others.

- Doing customer research interviews is the way to gaining a deeper understanding of your users.

Action Items to Improve Your User Onboarding

- Go through the five steps to do user interviews in Appendix I

  i.   Select and contact interview subjects.

  ii. Prepare a JTBD interview script.

  iii. Conduct the interview.

  iv. Transcribe and organize the interview scripts.

  v.   Gather then insights and implement them.

- Summarize the findings from the user interviews using the User Success Canvas at productled.com/user-success

Refine Your Onboarding Success Milestones

If you do not know where you are going, every road will get you nowhere.

- Henry A. Kissinger

oogle Maps can be quite a marvel. The vast majority of the time, it gets us where we need to go without having to think about it. We just plug in our destination, and boom, we're there. So many of us have become so reliant on it that when it fails, everything goes awry.

I experienced this firsthand with my wife Joanna on a road trip from Toronto to Montreal. Unfamiliar with the streets of Montreal, I relied heavily on Google Maps to find our hotel. Lo and behold, my phone lost signal after exiting an underground tunnel, and I received that dreaded error message, "GPS lost signal."

We ended up driving over a bridge that led to the US-Canada border. That wouldn't be so bad if we both had our Canadian passports, but we didn't!

Immediately, we both started to freak out. How are we supposed to explain to the Canadian Border Agents that we're not illegal immigrants trying to sneak into the United States of America, a.k.a. the land of the free?

Of course, we completely overreacted. The Canadian Border Services Agency officer we spoke with was understanding. After showing him our Ontario driver's license and explaining the Google Maps failure, he laughed it off. All we had to do was exit on a ramp that led us back to where we needed to go.

This is a harmless story, where not knowing your destination can lead you down the wrong path. But it doesn't always end well, especially with the cross-functional, highly visible effort of improving user onboarding.

By now, you should have a clear picture of what your users' desired outcomes are along with the functional, emotional, and social jobs they are hiring your product for. You should also now know the four progress-making forces that influence the decision to adopt or drop the product.

The next step is to define what success looks like for your user onboarding experience. There are three moments that matter the most to measure onboarding success:

1. When users complete the signup process.
2. When users experience the value of a product for the first time.
3. When they begin to use it consistently.

These three success criteria are tied to key milestones in the user onboarding: the Moment of Value Perception, Moment of Value Experience, and Moment of Value Adoption.

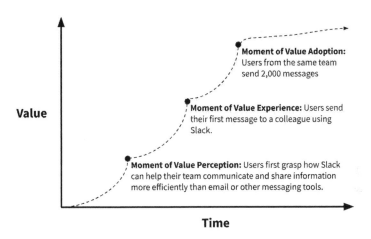

Success Criteria #1: The Signup

The first onboarding success criteria is getting users to complete the signup process. It *may* be a signal of a user's interest. The higher the friction is during the signup process, the higher the signal of interest.

For example, if you require a credit card upfront before someone can start a free trial (a.k.a. an opt-out free trial), you'll likely get fewer but higher-quality signups who are more likely to convert. Based on my experience, the trial-to-paid conversion rate of opt-out trials is as high as 60%.[32]

On the other hand, for opt-in trials that don't require credit card upfront, you'll likely increase your signup rate, but your trial-to-paid conversion rate could be as low as 5%.[33] If your intent is to get more people to try your product, the best option is to make your signup process as frictionless as possible. This means not requiring credit card details upfront with no strings attached. You'll get more people to try your product, but you have to qualify them better and try to win more of them.

Regardless of whether you have an opt-in or opt-out signup experience, a stronger signal of onboarding success is when users first experience the product's value.

Success Criteria #2: The First Strike

The second onboarding success criteria is helping users achieve their desired outcome, or Customer Job, as quickly as possible.

In Wes Bush's Bowling Alley Framework, this event is called the "First Strike." In 10-pin bowling, this happens when all ten pins are knocked down with a bowling ball. (We'll go deeper into the Bowling Alley Framework in the next chapter.)

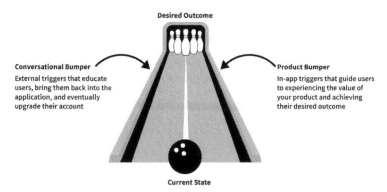

In user onboarding, the First Strike is a necessary product action users must take to accomplish their desired outcome or Customer Job. Let me give some examples.

- For Canva, it's exporting or sharing a finalized design.

- For Zoom, it's hosting or attending a Zoom meeting.
- For eCommerce stores, it's the first purchase of a product.

For some companies, this First Strike isn't so obvious. Think about Facebook. What's their First Strike? Is it a user liking, sharing, or commenting on posts?

Since those actions require users to have a few Facebook friends, the most important product action is to add a friend. That's why Facebook prompts new users to connect with friends as quickly as possible. This happens early on in their onboarding process.

For "all-in-one" products that solve many problems, recognizing the First Strike is even more tricky. Imagine identifying the First Strike for a Swiss Army knife. Is it the knife, pen, screwdriver, compass, scissors, saw blade, fire starter, or laser pointer?

Many all-in-one B2B SaaS products can essentially be considered digital Swiss Army knives. How do you determine the First Strike in these cases?

This is where context and segment matter. Depending on the context of use and the segment, there could be different First Strikes. For example, users can accomplish a lot with Intercom:

- Guide customers through their first steps, as well as highlight what's new with product tours.
- Build mobile carousels to onboard new app users.
- Create smart bots to qualify visitors on a website.
- Connect with website visitors and answer their questions in real-time.
- Manage customer support requests and questions.

- Make it easy for customers to serve themselves by sharing relevant help articles.

So, what is Intercom's First Strike?

It's hard to decipher at first glance. But by segmenting Intercom's users, you learn that users hire Intercom for three core Customer Jobs, all aligning with their three product lines:

- Conversational Support product: provides human, self-serve, and proactive support to increase customer satisfaction. A possible First Strike for this Customer Job is the first time users respond to and resolve a customer request.

- Conversational Engagement product: increases the engagement and product adoption with targeted in-app and outbound messages. A possible First Strike for this Customer Job is the first time users respond to an in-app or outbound message.

- Conversational Marketing product: acquires new customers quicker by responding to questions from prospects in real-time. A possible First Strike for this Customer Job is the first time users respond to a question from a website visitor.

As you can see, the First Strike is closely tied to your product's Customer Job (or Jobs, for more complex products). It's the first measure of success that new users are on the right track.

Success Criteria #3: The Tipping Point

The second measure of success is the moment users start using a product consistently.

One of the end goals of onboarding is to help users embrace new habits with a product. Habit-forming user onboarding requires users to experience the value of a product more than once. If new users have used the product enough times, they're more likely to continue with it going forward.

As mentioned in Chapter 1, for Slack, a team is not successfully onboarded until they've sent not one, not 10, but 2,000 messages. It's at this threshold where they've found the teams who are likely to continue using it.

This milestone is called **The Tipping Point**. It's when people start to transform from a skeptical user to someone who regularly uses the product. In other words, they've embraced the product and are very unlikely to return to their old habits.

Since this onboarding success metric is a *leading indicator* of user retention and product adoption, I call this the **Product Adoption Indicator,** or PAI for short. It's an early but strong signal that users are likely to continue using a product going forward.

This concept is not new—others call this the "magic number." Here are some well-known examples:

- At Facebook, users who add seven friends in 10 days are more likely to continue using Facebook.[34]
- In the early days of Twitter, the rule "Users who follow 30 people" was a retention and growth driver.[35]
- At Dropbox, users who added a file in one Dropbox folder on one device were more likely to add more files to their Dropbox.

Notice that the PAIs for each of these products are closely tied to retention.

Once users reach this point, you've set them up for success. They're now ready to take the next step in the product's customer journey. They've completed the initial loop of the user onboarding process: they've perceived, experienced, and adopted your product for the first time.

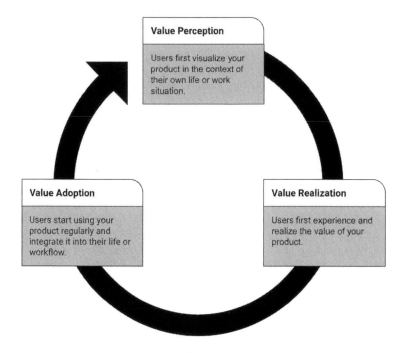

Good PAIs have a few common characteristics:

1. **PAIs should be leading indicators of user retention**: The PAI is the onboarding team's "canary in the coal mine," which means it provides early warning signs for miners of dangerous gases in a coal mine. With PAIs, you can predict with some confidence early on the likelihood of users sticking around to continue using a product. In other words, they're a strong signal that users have started forming a habit of using the product.

2. **PAIs should focus on the repetition of one key product engagement action**: One of the goals of user onboarding is to help new users build habits using a product. Since repetition is key for building habits, users need to use the

product a few times before it finally clicks for them. The PAI is tied to the product's desired outcomes or Customer Jobs (i.e., when a team has sent 2,000 Slack messages).

3. **PAIs should be easy to understand and communicate with others**: PAIs should be simple enough to remember and communicate with the entire company. Facebook employees "talked about nothing else" but seven friends in 10 days; it was their single, sole focus.[36] Instead of layering several user actions into the PAI, such as the number of likes, comments, and status updates, the company emphasized simplicity so it's easy to remember and share within the organization.

4. **PAIs should be time-bound**: Ideally, you want users to complete the PAI within a specific timeframe. With Facebook, it's adding seven friends in *10 days*. Slack's and Twitter's PAIs are not time-bound. But, having a timeframe can help your team identify if new users are off-track so you can adjust the user onboarding accordingly.

5. **PAIs should come early in the user's journey**. You want the ability to identify whether new users are on the path to success as early as possible. If the PAI occurs weeks later after signing up, you'll have fewer data points since many of those users will have already churned.

The Five Steps To Determine Your PAI

There are five steps to establishing a company's PAI.

I'll be using Whatsapp as an example for this exercise. **All data used below are fictional and used for instructional purposes only.**

With the steps below, I'm also assuming that you have product and user data to perform the steps below to determine your PAI. For new products with little to no data, these steps would not be applicable; first, focus on getting as many users as possible to experience the product's value (success criteria #2).

1. Get a baseline measurement of your retention.

As previously discussed, one result from good onboarding is a lift in retention rate. Before making any changes to the user onboarding, you'll want to first define what retention looks like.

One way to do this is to perform a cohort analysis using a retention chart and curve. This reflects the percentage of users who come back and perform any action with a product several days or weeks after signing up.

With analytics tools like Mixpanel or Amplitude, you should have readily available reports to visualize a product's retention curve. You could also calculate this metric by manually using Excel or Google Sheets.

For example, let's say 12,481 users downloaded your app on January 1, and you want to calculate the user retention rate for the first seven days. You need to track:

1. New users who signed up on January 1. This is Day 0 in the retention chart.

2. Users from January 1 who were active from Day 1 to Day 7.

Next, you need to divide the number of returning users by the total number of users, then multiply by 100.

$$\frac{\text{Number of returning users at the end of the time period}}{\text{Total number of users at the beginning of the time period}} \times 100 = \text{User retention rate}$$

Out of the 12,481 users who started on January 1, only 3,506 end up returning on January 2.

Day 1 retention is: $(3,506/12,481)^*100 = 28.1\%$.

Repeat the same process for the remaining days to calculate your retention table:

SEGMENT	USERS	DAY 0	DAY 1	DAY 2	DAY 3	DAY 4	DAY 5	DAY 6	DAY 7
⚫ All users	12,481	100.0%	28.1%	17.9%	20.6%	22.7%	18.7%	15.3%	15.1%
Jan 01	12,481	100.0%	28.1%	17.9%	20.6%	22.7%	18.7%	15.3%	15.1%

Plot this on a chart, with the days on the horizontal axis and the retention rates are on the vertical axis. By doing this, you can calculate the baseline retention curve for your current user onboarding experience.

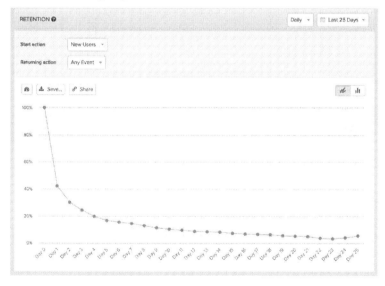

2. Create a PAI hypothesis.

Once you've identified the baseline retention curve, it's time to create a hypothesis about your retention indicator. It should look something like this:

If new users perform at least X number of **[the one key product action]** *during the first* **Y days/weeks** *of signing up, they're more likely to continue using our product after* **Z days/weeks**.

To create your own, let's back up to break it down:

- **Perform at least X number of [one key product action]:** User onboarding is about building habits. Habits are built with repetition. That's why users need to perform a minimum number of "Strikes" for the PAI. The one key product action for Whatsapp is to send a message. Set a target for new Whatsapp users to send three messages on the day of signing up.

- **During the first Y days/weeks of signing up:** For most products, the day new users sign up is critical. You want them to accomplish the key product action by then. For B2B products like HubSpot, it might take a week to accomplish the one key product action since it requires time to set up.

- **Continue using our product after Z days/weeks:** For this, take a look at your retention curve and find the point when it starts to flatten out. In this example, only 5% of users continue to use it after 21 days. But the retention rate holds steady after those first 21 days. Therefore, our PAI hypothesis would be: to drive users to continue using Whatsapp for 21 days because that's when they're likely to continue using it.

The final hypothesis for this example is:

If new Whatsapp users send at least three messages on the day of signing up, they're more likely to continue using it after 21 days.

3.   Gather data to validate your hypothesis.

What we're looking for here is to maximize the overlap between the following two segments:

1.   Users who continue to use Whatsapp after 21 days.
2.   Users who have sent at least X messages on the first day of signing up.

Another way to visualize this is by using a Venn diagram. The idea is to maximize the surface area between the segment of users who continue using Whatsapp after 21 days and the segment of users who have sent at least X messages on the first day of signing up.

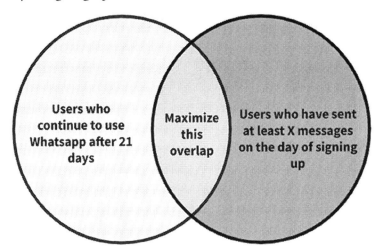

If you take a look at the segment of users who have sent at least nine messages on the day of signing up, many might continue to use Whatsapp after 21 days.

But there could be quite a few retained Whatsapp users who don't meet that number. In this case, the threshold for the PAI is too high. This is because we want to identify the *minimum* number of messages that also correspond to users who continue to use Whatsapp after 21 days.

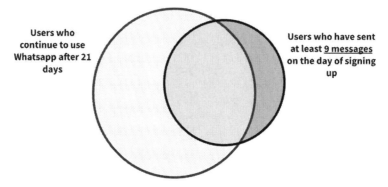

On the other end, most users who send at least one message on the day of signing up did not continue using Whatsapp after 21 days. In this case, the threshold is too low.

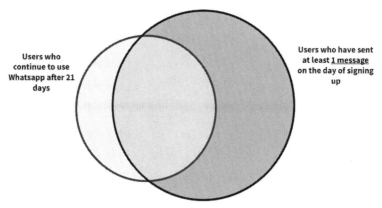

The goal is to find the sweet spot that maximizes the overlap between these two segments. To do this, we want to gather data for three segments:

1. Users who continue using Whatsapp after 21 days but did *not* send at least **X** messages on the day of signing up.

2. Users who continue using Whatsapp after 21 days *and* send at least **X** messages on the day of signing up.

3. Users who did *not* continue using Whatsapp after 21 days but *did* send at least **X** messages on the day of signing up.

This process is repeated for one, two, three, and so on. Here's what you'll see if you set this up in a table on a spreadsheet.

Messages Sent On Day of Signing Up	# Of Users Retained But Didn't Send At Least X Messages	# Of Users Retained AND Sent At Least X Messages	# Of Users NOT Retained But Sent At Least X Messages	Percent Overlap
1	163	457	1320	23%
2	340	301	670	23%
3	498	298	460	24%
4	603	257	345	21%
5	653	178	235	17%
6	676	127	164	13%
7	698	129	151	13%

Here you can see that users who sent at least three messages on the day of signing up have the biggest overlap with users who continue using Whatsapp after 21 days.

That's why Whatsapp's PAI is: **three messages sent on the day of signing up because they're likely to continue using it going forward.**

You can further visualize this using bar graphs. From this visual, it's clear that this has the biggest overlap between the two segments.

At Least X Messages Sent On Day of Signing Up	Retained User vs. Overlap vs. Users Who Sent At Least X Messages
1	28%
2	23%
3	24%
4	21%
5	17%
6	13%
7	13%

4.   Compare the retention curves and validate the PAI.

Next is to verify the PAI by comparing the retention curve of users who sent at least three messages on the day of signing up with the baseline retention.

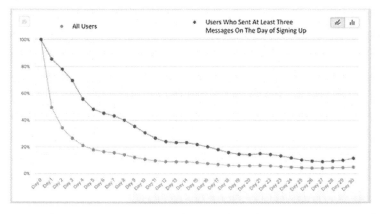

The retention curve indicates that the retention rate of users who sent at least three messages on the day of signing up is **almost double** the retention rate of your baseline rate for all users after 21 days.

If you're up for it and have the data chops, you can do a Logistic Regression.[37] This is beyond the scope of this book and requires a level of understanding of correlation and regression analysis. If you're interested, I've provided a link in the Suggested Resources section of this book.

5. Communicate your PAI.

Finally, once you've explored the data, ran some regressions, and verified that your model works, you're ready to explain it to others. The intention is to make it dead simple to talk about.

Communicate this to the marketing and sales teams to ensure they're not just pursuing signups. They should also focus on reaching the Moment of Value Adoption and achieving the PAI. Also, ask the sales and customer support teams to offer a higher level of support and care for these users.

This is exactly what Wave, a company that provides financial services and software for small businesses, did. After identifying their PAI, the whole organization adopted it as a measure of user success. Other teams joined in, including the demand gen team, to focus on channels and acquisition strategies that increase signups to reach the PAI.

It's important to note that PAI is just a term. Other companies may call it differently. Wave calls it the first activation event or FAE for short. Others call this "tier one" signups or leads. Whatever you end up naming it, make sure it's communicated often and adopted by your entire organization.

Product Qualified Leads and the PAI

It's worth touching on how the PAI relates to a product qualified lead (PQL). Are the PAI and the PQL the same metric?

Unlike Marketing Qualified Leads (MQLs), which base buying intent on arbitrary factors like email opens, whitepaper downloads, and webpage visits, PQLs are users who have achieved meaningful value in a product. It's often used as a way to identify high-value users to help the sales and support teams discover which users they should focus their efforts on.

Whereas the PAI focuses on one key product action so that it's easy to communicate within the organization, the PQL could involve multiple product engagement metrics. This includes but is not limited to the following:

- The number of times the user has returned to a product.

- The number of other features that the user has tried out.

- How soon the user tries out the other features after signing up.

To answer the question, yes, a PQL *could* be the same thing as a PAI, but it doesn't have to be. It really depends on the organization and whether the resources are available to provide high-touch support to more leads. If the resources are there, consider lowering the requirements for a PQL and set it for the moment users achieve their desired outcome for the first time. (We'll get into PQLs and the sales-assisted onboarding process in Chapter 10.)

Let's circle back to Slack for a minute. By now, we know Slack's PAI is when a team sends 2,000 messages. If there are only a handful of sales and support personnel at Slack, they could set the PQL equivalent to the PAI. But if they went on a hiring spree of sales and support folks, they could lower that bar and set it to the first time a team sends ten messages. At that level, there will be more PQLs the sales team can pursue.

Visually, if you look at a continuum of user engagement within your product, where one end is the moment users sign up and the other end is the moment users achieve the PAI, the PQL could be anywhere in between.

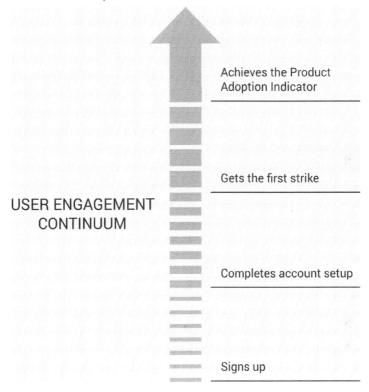

USER ENGAGEMENT
CONTINUUM

Achieves the Product
Adoption Indicator

Gets the first strike

Completes account setup

Signs up

Implementing a Product Analytics Tool

Everything we've talked about in this chapter assumes that you're measuring and tracking key product engagement metrics. This means going beyond a basic Google Analytics (GA) implementation.

GA was built to analyze marketing spend and was never meant to accommodate the depth and sophistication of a modern customer journey. Unless you define and implement events ahead of time, you can't measure product engagement. Even then, GA aggregates the data, so it's not possible to determine the *value* specific users are receiving from a product.

To measure the success of your onboarding experience, it's important to collect deeper insights and actionable information from your users. This can only come from detailed knowledge about how they interact with what you've built. When you have evidence regarding the specific actions of users and what they like best, you can engage them longer, further upsell them, and keep them happy so they come back time and again.

Whether it's Mixpanel, Heap Analytics, Amplitude, Pendo, or another product analytics tool, it is important to track meaningful product events and metrics.

For example, the key product engagement metrics for a B2B productivity tool could be:

- Projects created
- Tasks completed
- Team members added
- Comments left
- Files uploaded
- Projects completed

For a social networking application, key product engagement metrics could be connections made, published content, posts liked, and comments made.

The point is that your product is unique. Identify the key product engagement metrics that are important to your product.

Then implement a product analytics tool to track those metrics for each individual user.

What's Next

Once you've identified the PAI, the next step in the EUREKA framework is to evaluate your new users' journey. We're about to break down the user onboarding experience step-by-step to identify anything that could be limiting users from achieving your product's PAI.

Chapter 6 Summary

- There are two moments that matter the most in measuring the success of a user onboarding experience:
  i.   When users experience the value of a product for the first time.
  ii. When they begin to use it consistently.
- The first onboarding success criteria is when users achieve their desired outcome or Customer Job.
- The second measure of success is the moment users start using a product consistently.
- The Product Adoption Indicator (PAI) is a leading indicator of user retention and product adoption. It's an early but strong signal that users are likely to continue using a product going forward. Here are some well-known examples:
  i.   At Facebook, users who add seven friends in ten days are more likely to continue using Facebook.

ii.   In the early days of Twitter, the rule "Users who follow 30 people" was a retention and growth driver.

iii. At Slack, teams who have sent 2,000 messages are 93% more likely to continue using it going forward.

- Good PAIs have a few common characteristics:

i.   PAIs should be leading indicators of user retention.

ii.   PAIs should focus on the repetition of one key product engagement action.

iii. PAIs should be easy to understand and communicate with others.

iv.   PAIs should be time-bound.

v.   PAIs should come early in the user's journey.

Action Items to Improve Your User Onboarding

- Go through the five steps to determine your PAI.

i.   Get a baseline measurement of your retention.

ii.   Create a PAI hypothesis.

iii. Gather data to validate your hypothesis.

iv.   Compare the retention curves and validate the PAI.

v.   Communicate your PAI.

- Review your product analytics and identify where you're losing most new users in your user onboarding.

Evaluate Your Onboarding Path

> *Clutter is the official language used by corporations to hide their mistakes.*
>
> – William Zinsser

One of my dream cars is the Porsche Carrera GT. It can go 0 to 100 km/h in 3.57 seconds, all thanks to its 603 horsepower engine and curb weight of about 3,000 pounds.

Compare that with my current car, a Toyota Corolla, which has a 132 horsepower engine and weighs about 3,100 pounds. Not only does the Porsche have four times more horsepower than my Corolla, but it also weighs almost 100 pounds less!

The Porsche Carrera GT is a perfect example of how to make a car drive faster. First, increase the power the engine produces. Second, remove any unnecessary items to make the car as light as possible.

The second option is often the easiest, fastest, and cheapest way to speed up a car. Rip out the sound system, remove the bits of junk from the trunk, and (if you really have the need for more speed) pull out the rear seat. The 100-pound weight loss will make the car accelerate a tiny bit quicker.

The same can be said of user onboarding. When it's bloated with too many unnecessary steps, new users will abandon an app and leave it for good. Users have little to no patience to read long directions and no time for steep learning curves. The default is to find the easiest and quickest path. That's why the First Strike needs to be hit as quickly as possible.

In this chapter, we'll map out and evaluate the path for new users to ensure every step in the early stages of your customer's journey is as efficient and effective as possible.

The Straight-Line Onboarding

In the previous chapter, I introduced Wes Bush's Bowling Alley Framework and the concept of the First Strike—when first-time users achieve their desired outcome. In 10-pin bowling, that's when all of the pins are knocked down with a bowling ball. It sounds straightforward, right?

In reality, it's more complicated than that. The narrow oiled bowling lane is 41.5 inches wide, and the ten pins are 60 feet away. On both sides of this lane are gutters.

The goal is to roll a heavy ball straight down the lane to knock down as many pins as possible. A "strike" is when all of the pins are hit on the first try. A "spare" is when no pins are left standing after the second round.

If you're new to bowling, you'll quickly realize how hard (and frustrating!) it is to hit any of the pins. Chances are, the majority of your balls will end up in the gutter.

That's where gutter bumpers come into play; they block balls from falling into the gutter to give you a better chance of hitting some of the pins.

When it comes to user onboarding, bumpers help new users achieve their First Strike. Bumpers include conversational triggers (such as onboarding emails, SMS, browser notifications) and in-app triggers (such as welcome messages, product tours, and progress bars). I'll be covering these bumpers more in the next chapter.

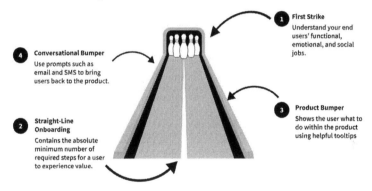

1 **First Strike**
Understand your end users' functional, emotional, and social jobs.

4 **Conversational Bumper**
Use prompts such as email and SMS to bring users back to the product.

3 **Product Bumper**
Shows the user what to do within the product using helpful tooltips

2 **Straight-Line Onboarding**
Contains the absolute minimum number of required steps for a user to experience value.

For now, let's identify the path that will help users achieve their First Strike. If you've watched professional bowlers, you'll notice how they curve the ball down the lane. This allows them to find the sweet spot that results in a strike. This is for pros, though. Beginners need to learn how to roll the ball straight down the lane first.

In user onboarding, this is called *Straight-Line Onboarding*. It's the minimum number of steps users need to take to achieve their First Strike. In my experience, most onboarding experiences are anything but a straight line. Well over 30% of them are superfluous and end up creating more friction for new users than necessary.

Creating a Straight-Line Onboarding experience is critical in getting more users to experience a product's value. You're in a race against time.

The goal is to decrease the *time-to-value* (TTV), the amount of time it takes a new customer to realize the value of a product. A short TTV means customers receive a faster return on their investment of time—and that means they are more likely to stick around!

This is exactly what the UserGuiding team found after they've removed unnecessary steps in their product's onboarding:

As soon as we removed the unnecessary info and directed the focus of our onboarding process to our Chrome extension, where the most of UserGuiding's value lies, we've seen our conversion rates almost double.

- Osman Koc, Co-founder of UserGuiding

With this in mind, here are three steps to building your own Straight-Line Onboarding experience.

How To Build Your Straight-Line Onboarding

To help you visualize this, I'll be going through the steps to develop the Straight-Line Onboarding of a fictional online party invitation tool that I'll call *PartyParrot.*

1. Map out your onboarding path

The first step is to sign up for your own product as if it's your first time. It's probably been a while since you've done that. More likely than not, it's been a while since *anyone* in your company has done that.

The goal is to come in with a fresh perspective and map out each step in the user experience *before* they become highly engaged users. To do this, you'll want to go beyond filling in the form on your site. Go through the motions of signing up to study the first impression of your product, whether that's a Google search, paid ad, blog post, or email invitation.

Since our online party invitation tool is fictional, let's start by looking at how Canva shows their design templates.

Someone might discover it by Googling, "Instagram post design template."

The very first result on the search engine results page (SERP) is a landing page dedicated to Canva's Instagram post templates.

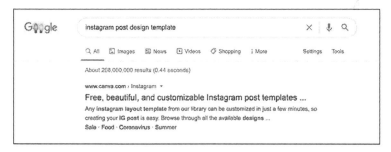

This link leads to a page with several Instagram post templates.

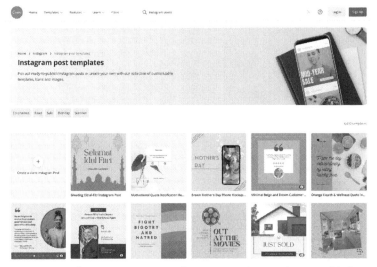

From there, users can select a template, edit it, add their own photos, and then download their masterpiece.

And voila, just like that, they've achieved their First Strike.

These first few touchpoints are key for users to experience the wonder of Canva for the first time. Here's the entire onboarding path from a Google search:

1. Search for "Instagram post design template"

2. Click on Canva's landing page

3. Select an Instagram template

4. Edit the Instagram design template

5. Add your own photos

6. Download the image

Notice how the first two steps aren't even part of the website; they both occur on the SERP. Don't forget that user onboarding doesn't typically start on a website. It begins with the very first touchpoint.

Another remarkable aspect about Canva's onboarding path is that users don't have to sign up at all to experience Canva's First Strike; their growth team has clearly optimized their user onboarding experience.

Now it's your turn: document every step that's required for users to achieve your product's First Strike. Be sure to reference every field that you're asking users to complete, including each button they need to click. I also recommend taking a screenshot of every step so you can refer to it later (you'll need this for later steps in the framework).

If you're doing this with the onboarding team in a room, you can use sticky notes and markers. Write down each step in one sticky note. For this exercise, consider each field a user has to fill out as an onboarding step. So if there are 10 fields on a signup page, that's 11 steps, including clicking on the submit button.

If your team is remote, you can use tools like Trello, Notion, or Miro. I've listed out every step in Canva's onboarding process with Trello at bit.ly/canva-path.

For the remaining steps, I'll use PartyParrot as an example. Let's say the current onboarding path from their website looks something like this:

1. Enter email address
2. Enter name
3. Enter password
4. Click "Create Account"
5. Confirm email address
6. Sign back in
7. Click "Create New Invitation"
8. Select a party invitation template
9. Add an image for the party
10. Add the description of the party
11. Add the date and time for the party
12. Add the location of the party
13. Save the online invitation
14. Add each email address of your friends
15. Send the online party invitation

2. Evaluate each step.

The next step is to evaluate each onboarding step for three components:

a) Necessity
b) Ease
c) Simplicity

A) Necessity: remove or delay any steps that don't lead to the First Strike

Each step in the onboarding path is yet another opportunity for users to drop off. Go back to your onboarding path and evaluate if the value of each step outweighs the risk they pose of a drop-off. Any steps that add more friction for users to achieve the First Strike should be removed or delayed.

Use green, yellow, and red labels to easily identify where each step falls in the onboarding process:

- **Green labels** are steps that are absolutely necessary for new users to achieve the First Strike. I.e., asking for an email address during the signup process.
- **Yellow labels** are steps that can be delayed after the First Strike, like setting up an advanced feature or running split tests.
- **Red labels** are steps that can be removed completely. This could be adding a backup email address or asking for a nickname when setting up their account.

Do this step collaboratively with the onboarding team.

Ask each team member to label every step on their own. Then, go through each step together to identify which ones are necessary. Removing the red and yellow steps are imperative to building a Straight-Line Onboarding experience so more users achieve the First Strike.

Let's go back to PartyParrot and evaluate each step.

Does step five–confirming the email address–help new users accomplish their immediate goal of sending online invitations?

This step is one of the biggest onboarding conversion killers.

Working with a graphic design tool Snappa, we discovered this firsthand. About 30% of new users never confirmed their email addresses. Once we did some simple math, we realized that with the removal of this activation step from the beginning of the onboarding flow, we'd be able to generate a 6-figure annual recurring revenue (ARR) outcome. In less than a week of implementation, we started to see their monthly recurring revenue (MRR) grow substantially.

Monthly Recurring Revenue (MRR)

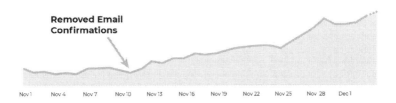

For those who still require new users to activate their email address before logging into the product, check your product analytics and see what percentage of new signups never touch foot in your product. Chances are 10% to 30% of new users never see the product because of this step.

So, let's get rid of step 5. As a result of this, users don't have to sign in again (step 6).

For step 9, does someone really need to add an image to send out party invites? One could argue that if the party invitation templates are well designed, users might not need to add a photo. Without any data, remove this for now.

Step 13, "save the online invitation," could be replaced with an autosave feature. It might seem small, but anything you can do to relieve people from performing another task could help improve new users achieving the First Strike.

Imagine the pain of manually entering the email address of each of your friends. That's why it makes more sense to replace Step 14 with a unique invitation link users can easily send out.

We've now narrowed the touchpoints down:

1. Enter email address
2. Enter name
3. Enter password
4. Click "Create Account"
   ~~Confirm your email address~~
   ~~Sign back in~~
5. Click "Create New Invitation"
6. Select a party invitation template
   ~~Add an image for the party~~
7. Add a description for the party
8. Add the date and time for the party
9. Add the location of the party
   ~~Save the online invitation~~
   ~~Add the email address of your friends~~
   ~~Send the online party invitation~~
10. Share ready-to-go party invitation link

Are there any steps in your onboarding that can be removed or delayed after the First Strike?

A word of caution: be careful with cutting too deep. Although friction slows down users, sometimes it may be helpful in successfully onboarding more people. For example, requiring users to input more data gives them more ownership.

This is what Wave (an invoicing and payroll software) does during the user onboarding process. It asks for a logo. Once they have it, they automatically identify the brand colors and update the invoice template to match the branding.

Some may think that this step is unnecessary and should be removed. But, after doing customer interviews, the Wave team found that this step got users excited about Wave:

> *During customer interviews, the customers we talked to that saw what their invoice would look like with Wave said, "Wow! This is great! This looks professional. It's beautiful." That gives them a lot of confidence that the product is good. Wave is something that they can trust.*
>
> - Vivek Balasubramanian, Director of Growth at Wave

This is the **IKEA Effect** in action. It's a cognitive bias in which consumers place a disproportionately high value on products they partially created or customized. The name refers to the furniture retailer IKEA, which sells items that require assembly. When people put in the effort to assemble furniture, they were willing to pay 63% more for it than the same pre-assembled one.[38]

So, before you cut a step out of your onboarding, ask yourself three questions:

1. Does it **direct** users to the next step in the onboarding process and get them closer to the First Strike? For example, Canva shows relevant design templates to users based on their response to the signup questions. Instead of offering too many choices, this step helps speed up the design process.

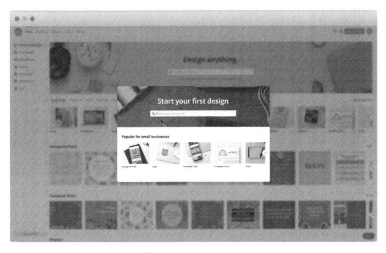

2. Does it **add** to and help personalize the onboarding experience for users? One of Canva's onboarding questions is, "What will you be using Canva for?" Based on this response, Canva suggests relevant designs and templates based on your needs that you saw in the previous example.

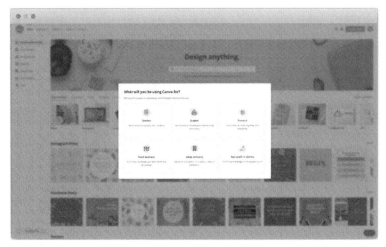

3. Does it **delight** users and get them excited about the product? Wave showing how its invoice looks like with a user's logo and brand colors is an example of this.

I call these questions the DAD test. (Yes, it's a riff on Rob Fitzpatrick's MOM test!)

B) Ease: reorganize steps from easiest to hardest

Baby steps are easier than large leaps. It's much more painless to commit to a smaller task at first and then gradually increase the difficulty. Imagine trying to run a marathon if you've never even run five miles in your life!

The Principle of Commitment and Consistency states that the smaller the initial ask from someone, the more likely they are to agree to bigger requests. This principle can be applied to user onboarding by reorganizing the steps from easiest to hardest.

HEY, an email app created by the team behind Basecamp, does a good job of applying this principle to their user onboarding. They focus on teaching users one step at a time, with each step gradually increasing in complexity and difficulty.

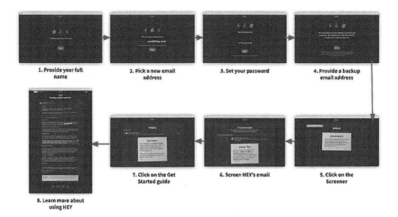

If you've played any video game like Super Mario, you've also seen this in action. Usually, they start with showing users' core actions. For Super Mario, this consists of moving forward, jumping, picking up a mushroom, and destroying a Koopa. As you become more familiar with the game, you learn new skills such as swimming, shooting fireballs, and running jumps.

The same principle can be applied to user onboarding. First, show core features of the product that users need to accomplish their Customer Job. As users become familiar with your product, unveil new options. This maintains simplicity for new users and brings power to advanced users.

Here's the onboarding path for PartyParrot again:

1. Enter email address
2. Enter name
3. Enter password
4. Click "Create Account"
5. Click "Create New Invitation"
6. Select a party invitation template

7. Add a description for the party

8. Add the date and time for the party

9. Add the location of the party

10. Share ready-to-go party invitation link

For steps 1 and 2: "Enter email address" and "Enter name," which one is an easier request to complete? Most likely, asking for a name. So flip them around.

We could probably take this a step further and ask users to create an account *after* they've already picked a party invitation template and filled in the details of their party. This is the **Sunk Cost Effect** in action. When people invest time, money, or effort into something, they're motivated to make it work. By investing in the customization of their party invitations, users are more likely to create their accounts.

With this concept in place, we can replace step 5 with, "Click 'Create an Account to Save Your Invite'"

1. Select a party invitation template

2. Add a description for the party

3. Add the date and time for the party

4. Add the location of the party

5. Click "Create an Account to Save Your Invite"

6. Enter name

7. Enter email address

8. Enter password

9. Click "Create Account"

10. Share ready-to-go party invitation link

We've now shrunk the onboarding path by 33% from 15 to 10 steps. Without unnecessary steps to bog new users down, more people will reach their First Strike!

For your onboarding, are there any steps you can reorganize from easiest to hardest?

C) Simplicity: show fewer options and break down complex signup and setup processes into smaller steps

There are situations where it's not possible to remove or delay the bottlenecks in the user onboarding experience. In that case, simplify as much as possible.

According to **Hick's Law**, the time it takes for users to make a decision increases logarithmically as you increase their number of choices. Thus, more choices lead to users becoming overwhelmed and abandoning the signup altogether. Take, for example, the following form with more than 20 fields. Would you sign up for this product?

For me, heck no! But I understand the intention. They're probably trying to learn more information about new users.

But, come on, did they really need to ask for your suffix? Really?!

Let's give them the benefit of the doubt and say all of those fields are absolutely necessary to experience the value of the product. Simplicity can still be achieved with a few tweaks.

First, consider a concept called **progressive disclosure**, where only a few essential options are shown to users, but a broader set is displayed upon request. In Shopify's signup process, only three fields are visible.

The moment you let Shopify know you're already selling online with another platform, a fourth field appears to ask which one you're using.

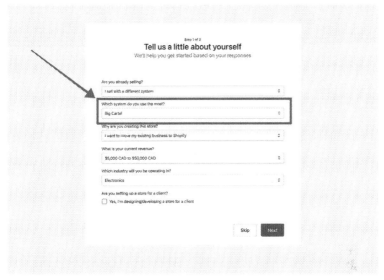

This works because of Hick's Law. Instead of cramming all of the information in one overlay page or setup wizard that almost everyone will ignore, guide users one step at a time by showing fewer options. Whatever information you present should be contextual, relevant, and immediate.

The second approach to simplifying complex forms is to break them up into multiple pages. Shopify also achieves this in their signup process. On the first page, they ask for four pieces of information (or three depending on your answer to the first question) about your eCommerce business:

- Are you already selling?
- What system do you use the most?
- What is your current revenue?
- What industry will you be operating in?

Once you complete these fields, the next step is to answer 10 additional questions, all related to the business address.

By using a multi-step signup process, users only see a few fields on the page at a time, rather than the 14 required fields needed to complete it. Notice there are almost double the number of fields in the second step (10 fields) than in the first step (4 fields).

This is another example of the Principle of Commitment and Consistency in action. By breaking down the signup page into two pages and moving the majority of the fields to the final page, Shopify's signup process is much more manageable.

Is there a way to show fewer options through progressive disclosure? Are there complex processes in your onboarding that could be broken up into smaller steps?

3.   Finalize your Straight-Line Onboarding.

Now, back to those color-coded labels. Once you've labeled each step in the onboarding path, gather those green ones together. This is the first iteration of your Straight-Line Onboarding because they are the steps users **need** to take to experience a product's value.

Again, here's the Straight-Line Onboarding for PartyParrot:

1. Select a party invitation template
2. Add a description for the party
3. Add the date and time for the party
4. Add the location of the party
5. Click "Create an Account to Save Your Invite"
6. Enter name
7. Enter email address
8. Enter password
9. Click "Create Account"
10. Share ready-to-go party invitation link

It's important to finalize this list with each team within your company. Everyone from product to engineering to customer support should have a say. Do they agree with each of the necessary steps for users to achieve their desired outcome? Would they add back in steps that you've removed or delayed? Would they remove any steps?

Segmenting Your User Onboarding

Now that you've built your product's Straight-Line Onboarding, I want to share one concept that's almost guaranteed to improve the performance of your user onboarding experience.

Ready?

Segmentation is conversion steroids for user onboarding.

Let me give you an absurd example to drive this point home.

Imagine if Disneyland cast members (a.k.a. their employees) forced visitors to follow a predetermined, one-size-fits-all schedule and route through the park. They've created it based on where the majority of the "average" guests go. The goal is to give visitors the full Disneyland experience as efficiently as possible.

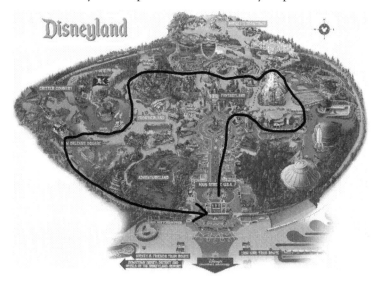

If this were the case, it would be pretty upsetting! The priorities of a couple on their honeymoon are different from a family with three kids. It doesn't make sense to force everyone to undergo the same schedule and route.

This scenario sounds absurd, right? (Don't worry, no cast members and Disneyland customers were harmed in this thought experiment!)

For most companies, their user onboarding is precisely this – a one-size-fits-all, linear experience for everyone. They've built their user onboarding for the "average" new user.

This might work with early-stage products, where that kind of focus helps channel all resources to reach product-market fit. But a product's features will inevitably grow, expand, and mature. Shoppers will sign up for many different reasons.

A product might accomplish different Customer Jobs for separate market segments. So instead of a one-size-fits-all experience, tailor the user onboarding for each Customer Job.

In the example with Disneyland, cast members can better highlight shows and rides based on the preferences of each customer. For a couple on their honeymoon, they might suggest romantic restaurants and shows. For families with young kids, they might suggest age-appropriate rides and attractions.

With this approach, you can highlight the right features at the right time, giving users the tools to execute each specific job. You can also better position the product as the solution to their needs.

When we apply this thinking to The Bowling Alley Framework, we can assign users to a bowling alley based on their jobs-to-be-done. Each alley is a segment, and different Conversational and Product Bumpers can be designed to help new users accomplish the job they hired your product to do.

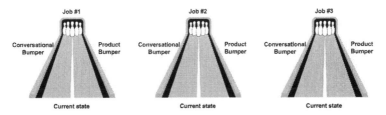

There are three main benefits of doing this:

1. Users learn what they need to in order for them to experience their First Strike.

2. You can get down to the specifics of how exactly your product can help them.

3. You can increase user motivation by sending targeted messaging based on each user's primary goal.

I provide a step-by-step guide to help identify your product's Customer Jobs by doing user interviews in Appendix I. For each Customer Job, repeat the three steps to build a Straight-Line Onboarding experience.

The Next Action

Even if we create the best possible experience for users, we're still going to see a lot of them stuck in the gutters; they'll never return to the product. Others will find themselves off-track. We need to plan for those detours.

We can do that with bumpers that keep users in a straight line. That's the next step in the EUREKA framework: keep new users engaged both inside and outside your product.

Chapter 7 Summary

- Straight-Line Onboarding is the minimum number of steps users need to take to achieve their First Strike.
- Here the three steps to build your Straight-Line Onboarding:
    i. **Map out your onboarding path.** Sign up for your own product as if it's your first time. Document every step that's required for users to achieve your product's First Strike. Be sure to reference

every field that you're asking users to complete, including each button they need to click.

ii. **Evaluate each step for necessity, ease, and simplicity.** Remove or delay any steps that don't lead to the First Strike. Reorganize steps from easiest to hardest. Show fewer options and break down complex signup and setup processes into smaller steps.

iii. **Finalize your Straight-Line Onboarding.** Everyone from product to engineering to customer support should have a say. Do they agree with each of the necessary steps for users to achieve their desired outcome? Would they add back in steps that you've removed or delayed? Would they remove any steps?

- Segmentation is conversion steroids for user onboarding.
- Tailor the user onboarding for each Customer Job so can highlight the right features at the right time, giving users the tools to execute each specific job.

Action Items to Improve Your User Onboarding

- Build your Straight-Line Onboarding using the steps from this chapter. You can download a fillable worksheet at productled.com/straight-line-onboarding.

Keep New Users Engaged

> *The mediocre teacher tells. The good teacher explains. The superior teacher demonstrates. The great teacher inspires.*
>
> – William Arthur Ward

D o you remember a teacher who made a difference in your life?

Even though you may not remember all the teachers you've had, I bet there were a few who made a lasting impression. They might have even influenced your career today.

For me, that was Mr. Drmanic, my physics teacher during high school. He was funny, brilliant, and explained complex physics concepts with a ton of energy. Above all, he cared about his students. At the start of the year, he'd always ask everyone what they wanted to be when they grew up. He then made a point to relate his lessons to the professions we announced to the class. He inspired me to major in math and computer science in university.

Mr. Drmanic's teaching approach is exactly what user onboarding needs – to educate, explain, and inspire users. It's crucial to find the right balance so that users are not overwhelmed or bored.

Once you've created your Straight-Line Onboarding, the next step is to add "bumpers" so users remain engaged and eventually adopt the product into their life or workflow.

So... how do you immerse new users into your product so they feel motivated and inspired?

This is where a useful framework called the **BJ Fogg Behavior Model** comes in.

The BJ Fogg Behavior Model

The BJ Fogg Behavior Model is the key to unlocking behavior change and product adoption for new users. Dr. BJ Fogg, behavioral scientist and founder of the Behavior Design Lab at Stanford University, created this model to facilitate behavior changes by adopting positive habits and letting go of unfavorable ones. It emphasizes three elements that must converge simultaneously for a behavioral switch to occur:

- Motivation (M): The desire or willingness to do the new behavior.
- Ability (A): The ease in doing the new behavior.
- Prompt (P): The cue or trigger to do the new behavior.

Together, these elements form the BJ Fogg Behavior Model:

If you plot Motivation and Ability on a graph, you'll see a curved smiling shape called the Action Line.

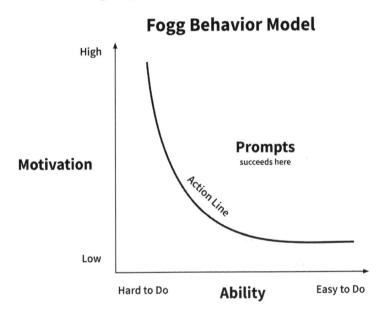

Behaviors that ultimately become habits will reliably fall above the Action Line. For example, let's say you're training for a marathon and aim to wake up at 6 a.m. every morning. Even with no running experience, you set an unrealistic goal of running a 10-mile run that first morning. It's a sure way to fail because this behavior falls below the Action Line.

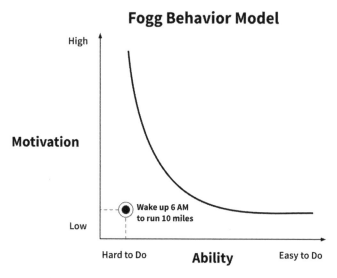

But, let's say you sleep in your running shoes and reward yourself with a chocolate banana smoothie after the run, all while setting a realistic goal of running two miles on the first day. Since you've increased the motivation and made it easier to get started, you're more likely to accomplish it.

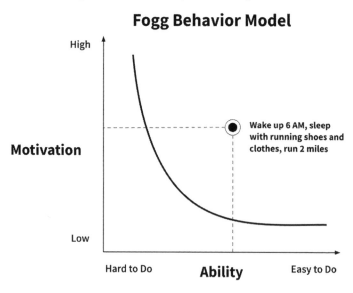

Now, how does all this relate to user onboarding?

Ultimately, you're not onboarding people to a product. You're onboarding them to a new way of accomplishing something, a new way of life. In essence, it's a behavioral switch for users. They have to let go of their old habits and adopt new ones.

If users are falling off during the user onboarding, the BJ Fogg Behavior Model provides a framework to boost those numbers:

1. Is the new behavior as easy to do?

2. Are users motivated to perform the behavior?

3. Are there prompts inside and outside the product to help users perform the desired behavior to complete the user onboarding?

In the Bowling Alley Framework, the Product and Conversational Bumpers should contribute to one or more elements in the BJ Fogg Behavior Model to either make the onboarding experience easier, increase the motivation of new users, or prompt them to do something.

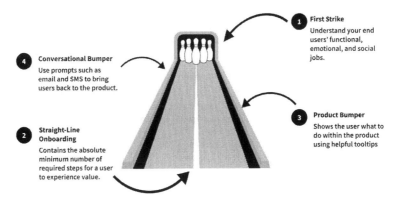

This chapter focuses on how you can use the BJ Fogg Behavior Model to keep users engaged both inside and outside a product. It's divided into three sections:

- Section 1: Learn how to use visual cues, empty states, and content templates to make user onboarding easier.

- Section 2: Discover different ways to increase your users' motivation inside and outside the product.

- Section 3: Create behavior-based prompts for user onboarding

  If you'd like to see an overview of the different types of Product and Conversational Bumpers, see Appendix II and III.

Section I: Make It Easy

If you want to change the behaviors and habits of users, you need to make the behavior as easy as possible to do.

One useful concept to measure how easy (or hard) user onboarding is for new users is **cognitive load**– the mental effort required to learn new information. You can think of cognitive load as the mental processing power needed to learn how to use and interact with a product. If the information exceeds the user's ability to handle it, it results in a **cognitive overload**.

From my experience, most user onboarding overwhelms new users with signup fields, product tours, pop-ups, in-app messages, checklists, tooltips, and more. If users feel overwhelmed, they'll experience cognitive overload and likely abandon the app altogether.

So, how do you avoid overloading users?

With Straight-Line Onboarding in place from the previous chapter, you're already halfway there. By now, you should have:

- Removed or delayed any unnecessary steps that don't lead to the First Strike.
- Reorganized the onboarding steps from easiest to hardest.
- Simplified the onboarding by showing fewer options while breaking down complex signup and setup processes into multiple steps.

You can take additional steps within your product to make for a remarkable first-time experience for new users that's both easy and effective.

1. Provide visual cues to guide them to the next onboarding step

At times, new users need a small clue on what to do next. Little cues or context changes can encourage users to make a certain decision. This can be as simple as an image that points users to the next step.

Basecamp adds some fun to their onboarding by using a cartoon character to point out where users complete the signup form.

Visual cues can also be Product Bumpers that guide new users to achieve their desired outcome.

Here's what a Product Bumper could look like:

- Product tours orient new users and help them find the fastest path to their first moment of value. Tours often walk users through a critical workflow or point out a few key steps that users might otherwise miss.

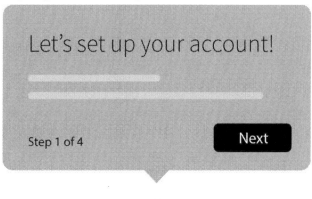

- Tooltips isolate elements such as form fields or buttons to guide a user through the account setup. Once a user completes a step, they are referred to the next one.

- Hotspots are often used to give a bit of contextual help to encourage new users to activate certain product elements or features. They can have unique pulsing animations to catch a user's eye. Hotspots are a nice alternative to tooltips because they are less invasive to users; they don't open automatically and can be easily ignored.

Check out this feature!

These are just a few examples of Product Bumpers. Others include checklists, progress indicators, and welcome messages (more on those later).

When using Product Bumpers, tours are usually a better bet than an unending blast of tooltips. They help users achieve the desired outcome through action instead of memorization. Canva does a good job of this by guiding users through four steps to download their first design.

Be careful of using Product Bumpers as a band-aid for bad user experience. One of my biggest pet peeves with product tours is that it's often used to point out all the bells and whistles of the app. They tell you *what* the button or feature does (i.e., "Click here to do X.") and not explain *why* they are important to help users achieve their desired outcome. When they're added on as an afterthought, product tours can do more damage by disrupting the momentum for users rather than getting them excited to use the product.

Regrettably, they have become deeply associated with user onboarding, to the point where many companies believe adding them will automatically improve it. This is flat-out wrong. Ironically, it's often a sign someone slapped on the onboarding experience without much thought or strategy.

2. Show a helpful empty state

When users are just starting out, they'll often see pages within a product without any activity, history, or data because it's their first time interacting with it. These moments are called **empty states.**

Empty states are often overlooked as a helpful way to guide users to achieving their First Strike. This happens because interfaces are typically designed with data already in place, so the layout looks clean and organized. So when users sign up for the first time, it can be disheartening to see a bunch of zeros and placeholder images on the main page, which is what you see when you sign up for Mailchimp, an email marketing platform.

Instead, you want to paint a picture of what it will look like once the user is actively using the product. Emphasize the value of taking action. Go beyond showing users the benefits of your app. Direct them to the desired action as well.

Take a look at Dropbox Paper's empty state. It describes how it can help you "brainstorm, review design, manage tasks or run meetings." There's a clear, primary call-to-action to direct users to begin using Dropbox Paper.

A word of warning: avoid using "dummy data" to generate fake activity and statistics in the empty areas. While it's tempting to cover empty states with fake data to bring the dashboard to life, it presents an entirely new problem of overwhelming users. You're opening up the door to questions such as:

- "Am I supposed to do something here, or should I just look at it?"
- "Where did this data come from?"
- "Where do I put in my data?"
- "How do I know it's my stuff that I'm looking at?"

There are times when "dummy data" can work: when it actively instructs instead of merely being seen. Basecamp does an excellent job of doing this to explain how their product works. Each piece actively guides you through using the product.

3. Provide templates, cheat sheets, and other resources

Content is like cheat codes to your onboarding. Templates, cheat sheets, and educational articles are often overlooked as a way to make it easier to onboard new users. They can help speed up the onboarding process because users don't need to start from scratch.

Let's say I give you a pen and a blank piece of paper. I ask you to write a 500-word story. Your brain starts churning and asks questions like:

- Should I write a love story? Or maybe a story about a hero who saves the day?
- Who are my main characters? Who or what is the antagonist of the story?
- Why is Ramli making me write a story?

It'll probably take several minutes before you start writing something down!

But let's say I provide you with a pre-written story. All you have to do is give a list of words to substitute for blanks in it. Your work is minimal and easy.

It's the same with onboarding. One way for users to quickly fill in empty states is to provide them with templates to copy and paste easily. There is no need to build from scratch.

For example, Instead of Canva dropping its users into an empty state, they prompt them to pick a template.

Assess the skills users need to achieve their desired outcome and then craft content around that to place in the empty state.

Userlist, a behavior-based customer messaging platform, does this well. When new users sign up, they're given a relevant integration guide, as well as a useful communication planning worksheet.

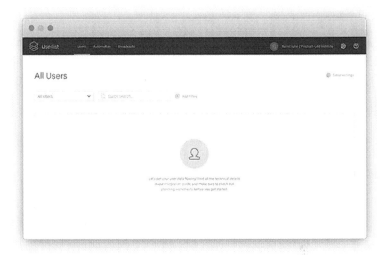

The Userlist team goes further by providing super simple copy-and-paste templates of emails and in-app messages users can use for onboarding.[39]

Since they know their audience so well, they're able to provide highly targeted content that speaks to the solution of their problem:

1. A behavior-based communication strategy to help onboard new users

2. Customizable full-text templates for every type of campaign across the entire customer lifecycle

So ask yourself this: for your user onboarding, are you able to provide templates, worksheets, or shortcuts to make it easier for new users to achieve their First Strike?

Section 2: Increase Motivation

Another element to building new habits is motivation. It's a major driving force of behavioral change. With enough motivation, you can change anyone's behavior, including your most critical users. You just have to find the right carrot to dangle in front of them, right?

It's not that simple. External rewards like money, fame, and praise sometimes actually work *against* people completing a task. Since they're only interested in the reward, they won't complete the task on their own initiative if it isn't there.

That's why I typically don't recommend incentives for users to complete the onboarding process. Rewards like trial extensions, badges, or branded stickers might encourage users to complete the onboarding, but those users might not be interested in the product itself; they're apathetic to the product and end up leaving.

What I *do* recommend is using Product and Conversational Bumpers to increase a user's intrinsic motivations. There are a few ways to do this:

1.   Speak to your users' desires

Often, onboarding teams approach the content of signup screens and onboarding elements like tooltips and product tours as a low priority—and it shows. Even if it's well-written, it's usually focused on product features rather than communicating the benefits of these features. This is a mistake.

The ultimate motivation is to show users how the product can help improve their lives. Every word in the entire user onboarding experience is an opportunity to speak to users' needs and desires. Use content to amplify the solution to their current pain points, calm their anxieties, and remind them they can overcome their existing habits.

For example, the third step in the signup process with Wave reminds new users of the value of their invoicing software. The copy reads, "Send professional invoices. Designed to get you paid 3x faster, with over \$24 billion in invoices sent each year."

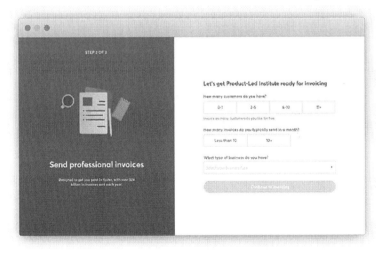

Wave's team knows that new users are still skeptical, so they use social proof to convince them Wave is the right tool. After all, who doesn't want to get paid three times faster?

Airbnb is a bit more subtle in how they do this.

When searching for a place to stay, Airbnb nudges users to add their date and number of guests.

Airbnb achieves two objectives here. First, they encourage visitors to enter their travel details so they can view more accurate pricing. Second, they warn users about tourism taxes which may be added at checkout so they're not surprised. This is an excellent example of how to address objections before they even come up.

Does the content in your user onboarding speak to the desires and needs of your users? Do you address the concerns, anxieties, and objections in your copy?

2.   Show them progress.

Like a workout partner pushing you to complete one more rep, encourage more users to complete the signup, setup, and onboarding process by showing them their progress. Use **progress indicators** to inform users of their status of completion (e.g., the percentage of steps that are left to complete). Chances are, you've seen this in action before.

Canva uses an indicator in their product tour to indicate where a user is in their four-step product tour.

LinkedIn uses a progress bar to show how to improve your "Profile Strength."

WHO'S VIEWED YOUR PROFILE

0 Your profile has been viewed by 0 people in the past 90 days.

0 You have shown up in search results 0 times in the past 90 days.

PROFILE STRENGTH

Beginner

Improve Your Profile Strength ›

Progress indicators appear mostly in signup flows, like in this three-step signup process from FullStory.

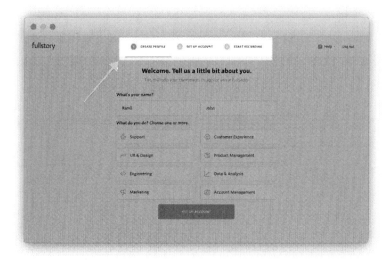

Place them wherever is most appropriate – Growthhackers adds it as an onboarding checklist during the account setup.

Progress indicators work so well because humans are wired to set goals, and we inherently feel good when we accomplish them. It turns out that when you finish a complex task, your brain releases massive quantities of endorphins.[40]

There's also an internal tension that occurs when a checklist or progress bar appears incomplete. This is called the **Zeigarnik**

Effect: when people feel the need to finish incomplete tasks. This is a massive win for user onboarding. Simply framing to-do items or a signup process as incomplete can be a huge win.

Do you tell users how far along they are in completing a set of tasks with progress indicators during the signup, account setup, and user onboarding of your product?

3. Welcome new users

Usually, we're more likely to say "yes" to requests from people we like and are attracted to, whether they're our closest friends or strangers.

But what exactly causes attraction? Persuasion science tells us there are three important factors. We like people who are similar to us, people who pay us compliments, and people who cooperate with us to attain mutual goals.

One way to harness this powerful principle into user onboarding is to welcome new users. Many may believe this introduction is a massive waste of time. But if you create a common bond, build a connection, and relate to a shared mission, it can be an enormous boost of motivation for new users.

It doesn't need to be anything fancy either. With a short video from their three founders, Userlist creates a bond with users thanks to the personal message.

Many products ignore this critical step. But imagine walking into a dinner party without the host greeting you and giving a tour. Most likely, you'd feel snubbed and hurt!

Welcome messages also set the tone. They give customers a sense of how they'll be treated during their relationship with the product. Personal videos are great at humanizing the experience while implying someone is personally involved in the users' success.

Fiverr's welcome message reads, "Welcome to Fiverr. You're now part of a global community of doers. Fiverr is a marketplace of talented online freelancers who pride themselves on getting it done for you. On time. On budget. Get everything from custom websites to fresh, original content, stunning graphics, and much more."

The call-to-action is, "Get Sh*t Done."

Fiverr does three things well here:

1. They welcome users to the "global community of doers" to emphasize the message that they are not alone.

2. They reiterate their value – helping to find freelancers who deliver projects "from customer websites to fresh, original content and much more" on time and on budget.

3. With the profanity in the primary call-to-action, their personality shines through. Fiverr knows their target audience is casual, so don't shy away from a little bit of profanity.

When writing welcome emails, consider setting expectations for upcoming content and giving instructions on how they can reach out for help. And for goodness sake, please don't use an email address people can't reply to, like with Fiverr's email from "no-reply@fiverr.com." Emails should be two-way communication and an opportunity for users to ask for help.

Are you welcoming users to your product? If you have a welcome message in place, are you creating a common bond, building a connection, and relating on a shared mission?

4. Celebrate their wins

After you've done the heavy lifting to acquire new users and guide them to the First Strike, don't throw it all away by assuming the job is done. It's essential to keep them interested in the product. By celebrating your customers' achievements, you can create a correlation between their success and your own.

The more users come to view your product as an ingredient in their own success, the more traction you'll have in the long term. When users achieve a meaningful milestone, congratulate them with an in-app message or email.

Once the first invoice is sent with Wave, a screen pops up that reads, "Congratulations! Get ready to see more invoicing goodness."

It doesn't end there. They then encourage new users to download the Wave mobile app to track invoices on the go. A field appears to enter a phone number with a CTA that reads, "Text me the link."

Did you notice how they phrase this? It's exactly what users want to know after sending an invoice (the tracking information). They've also made it easy to download the app by sending a text message with a direct link to it.

Also, consider sending congratulatory onboarding emails. Buzzsprout, a podcast hosting platform, congratulates users after publishing their first podcast episode. The email reads, "Congratulations from Buzzsprout! 1st episode published." The show's cover art is presented above the message, and they ask you to spread the cheer by sharing the good news on Facebook or Twitter.

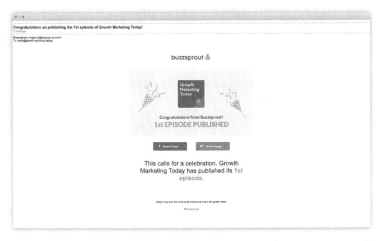

Another simple example is to add this after users upgrade their accounts. At Chess.com, they send an email as a reminder of all the benefits you receive once you become a premium member: unlimited access to chess lessons, an ad-free playing experience, as well as tools to analyze the games and more.

The onboarding team at Sprout Social takes it a step further by mailing new users a gift box of goodies, including a coffee mug, stickers, a thank you note, and more after they've completed the user onboarding process.[41] This grand gesture congratulates new users for achieving a milestone while delighting them enough, so they tell others about it.

For your user onboarding, have you identified the wins, milestones, and success moments to congratulate new users?

5. Use social proof

When people are uncertain, they'll look to the behaviors of others to determine their own. This is known as **social proof.** For instance, if we see a particular restaurant is always full, we're more likely to eat there.

Social proof is immensely important for user onboarding. Joel Klettke, Founder of Case Study Buddy, points out that it sets expectations, gives leads a comparison party to weigh themselves against, reinforces your messaging, and substantiates your claims.[42] It does so much at the same time.

We've already seen an example earlier from Wave. They emphasize in the third step of their signup process that, "over $24 billion invoices" with Wave are sent each year.

Add social proof to onboarding emails. This can be in the form of case studies, reviews, endorsements, or testimonials from happy customers.

Shopify uses a testimonial from Fred, Luca, and Danni to show how easy it is to start an eCommerce business: "Shopify let us build an eCommerce platform without having prior knowledge or allocating significant resources."

Social proof establishes trust for skeptical new users and increases motivation to hop on the train to your product.

From my experience, most products only include social proof on their landing pages. But you should be going beyond that:

- Use social proof as supporting copy near a CTA or at a point of friction.
- Use social proof to counter objections. What are the reasons someone might not convert?
- Use social proof to support the value of a product.
- Use social proof to humanize your marketing. A one-line testimonial from John Smith is meaningless. Put names to faces, list companies, link to their Twitter pages. Don't leave out social media.
- Use social proof in your in-app content and onboarding emails.

Are there steps in your user onboarding where you can add social proof?

Section 3: Create Behavior-Based Prompts

Prompts (or triggers) are one of the most powerful forces that shape our lives. Chances are you've encountered hundreds of prompts already today. You've probably barely noticed them.

- Your alarm goes off. So you wake up, brush your teeth, and then make coffee (in the same order every day).
- Your phone buzzes, so you check it for new notifications.
- You're hungry, so you eat lunch.

Whether you realize it or not, most habits start with a Prompt. Another way to put it – no prompt, no action.

In the user onboarding experience, prompts are critical during two moments:

1. To help users achieve their desired outcome and experience the value of a product soon after signing up.

2. To help users continue to use a product until they adopt it into their life and workflow.

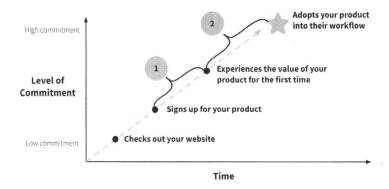

During the user onboarding journey, prompts can occur inside the app (product tours, checklists, tooltips, and other Product Bumpers) or outside of it (emails, SMS, phone notifications, and old-school direct mail). They're critical in creating an engaging environment for new users to learn how a product works and to decide if it's the right fit for them.

Often, when onboarding is added on as an afterthought, prompts become a crutch to mask poor UX design. Remember, the BJ Fogg Behavior Model states that Prompts only work if users have the necessary motivation and ability above the Action Line.

Successful and effective onboarding prompts have three qualities:

First, Prompts should be omnichannel, involving cohesive, thoughtful messaging across multiple channels that considers where users are in the onboarding journey. One of those channels should be email. That's because email remains surprisingly effective:

- It's accessible—most people have at least one email address.
- It's expected—people expect at least a welcome email.
- It's understood—it's a channel that's been around for years.

On top of that, email can help you stay top-of-mind and drive re-engagement, so users don't churn. When done well, onboarding emails can provide a gentle nudge to encourage users to act while helping them stay on track.

Second, Prompts should be personalized and timely. Avoid a purely time-based email flow at all costs. The problem with this approach is:

- It does *not* consider what the user has already done in your product.
- It does *not* personalize the emails to drive users to the next step in the onboarding process.

- It does *not* adapt to users needs, anxieties, and challenges.

To avoid coming across as annoying and spammy, trigger emails based on the actions users have or have not taken inside the product. This ensures the communication is both timely and relevant.

Third, Prompts should reiterate the value of your product. Remember that value is not determined by your company nor by the expansiveness of your feature set. Value is defined by your users based on their context of use.

That's why it's important to segment email flows based on the product's Customer Job. Since each user has unique friction points, a product may have multiple onboarding email flows, all based on specific user behaviors. However, I recommend starting with a single path and then adding sophistication to the onboarding email flow over time.

At ProductLed, we use a three-step process to use Prompts in the onboarding process. You can apply this process to all types of Conversational Bumpers, such as SMS text messages, browser notifications, in-app messages, direct mail, and more. Here's how to create a behavior-based onboarding communication plan.

Step 1: Identify the key milestones in your Straight-Line Onboarding

This could be:

- Right after users sign up, so you can welcome them.
- Critical onboarding steps users need to complete to experience the value of the product.
- The moment users achieve their First Strike.

- Before, during, and after the free trial period ends.

Here's the Straight-Line Onboarding users experience when they sign up for Canva from the homepage:

1. Click "Sign Up" on the homepage
2. On the "Get started" modal, click "Sign up with email"
3. Enter your full name
4. Enter your email
5. Enter your password
6. Click "Get started"
7. Select an option from "What will you be using Canva for?"
8. Click "skip" on "Try Canva Pro" modal
9. Click "skip" on "Add team member" modal
10. Select a template
11. Edit a template
12. Add your own photos
13. Click on download
14. Click on print, download, or share
15. Try "Canva Pro" for 30 days

From my perspective, there are seven key milestones in Canva's onboarding:

1. User signs up
2. Select a template
3. Edit a template
4. Add your own photos
5. Download design
6. Start Canva Pro Trial

7. Canva Pro Free Trial Ends

Step 2: Add behavior-based prompts based on the actions users take inside the product

The next step is to add behavior-based prompts to the Straight-Line Onboarding milestones.

Not all user journeys are the same. One visitor could sign up for the product and then immediately become distracted by a phone call. Others might sign up, play around with a few core features and decide not to convert.

By sending relevant emails filled with juicy content related to a user's specific needs, the product is kept at the top of mind and kickstarts their motivation to use it again.

Behavior-triggered emails also have the potential to take users further on in their onboarding journey. By sharing super-specific information at the right time, you're not at risk for repeating details they already know or that's ahead of their learning curve. Keep the emails resourceful, with one clear CTA that drives them back to actions they haven't yet finished.

There are a ton of powerful tools out there that can help you create behavior-based emails. For better segmentation, look for ones that target based on product and user data such as Intercom, Userlist, or ActiveCampaign.

To build a behavior-based onboarding email flow, look at the success path of your Straight-Line Onboarding milestones.

For each step, determine the information or content users might require to complete it.

Going back to the BJ Fogg Behavior Model, users need enough Motivation and Ability to complete the next step in the Straight-Line Onboarding. So, if they're getting stuck, it could be a lack of either one or both.

If they lack motivation, share content that amplifies the pain of their current situation. Reiterate the value of your product.

If it's a lack of ability, share relevant templates, resources, video tutorials, or educational articles. Also, remind them how to get in touch with the team for support.

Let's apply this process to Canva.

The first important onboarding step after users sign up with Canva is selecting a design template. Ask yourself, why might new Canva users *not* select a template? Maybe they lack inspiration. In that case, use an email to send relevant design templates or inspiration.

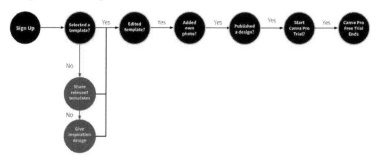

The next step in Canva's Straight-Line Onboarding is to edit a template. Once again, ask yourself why users might *not* edit a template they've selected. Maybe they're confused about how to do it. Perhaps they need help from the support team.

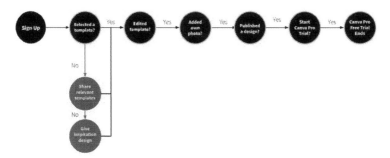

Repeat this process for the remaining milestones. And don't forget to send welcome messages!

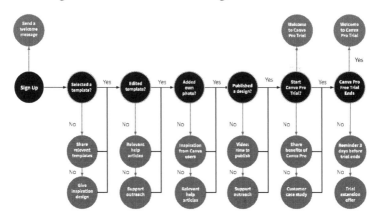

Here are some additional examples of other types of content you can send during the onboarding process. Take a peek at *Appendix II: Conversational Bumpers* for easy copy-and-paste templates.

- **Value-based emails** focus on communicating the functional, emotional, or social job of a product. How will your product make the user's life better?
- **Usage tips** are helpful nudges that direct users to take steps that will set them up for success.

- **Case studies** share customer success stories to inspire users to continue using the product and become paying customers. Share stories to overcome objections.
- **Trial expiration warning emails** remind users how many days are left in the trial period and emphasizes the value of upgrading to a paid account.
- **Trial extension emails** ask users if they want a trial extension. You'd be surprised how many trial extension requests end up turning into paying customers.
- **Sales touches** are when the sales or customer success teams reach out to users. These can be automated or manual emails. I'll talk more about the right time to send these types of emails in Chapter 10.

Step 3: Fill in the details

Remember to check out Appendix III for some copy-and-paste templates. Here are some best practices to consider when filling in the details to help you make the best of them.

1. **Set one primary CTA for each onboarding email.** This should be simple enough to do since each email in the behavior-based email flow corresponds to a key milestone in your Straight-Line Onboarding. Create clear, compelling CTAs for each email that effectively helps users complete the step they haven't finished yet.

2. **Make it personal.** Just because a brand targets enterprise customers doesn't mean the emails can't be fun. Avoid talking like a robot. Copy like "You're in!" or "Let the fun begin," or "Get the latest fashion — and help local charities"

are simple yet effective messaging that gives readers that "good feeling" when supporting your brand.

3. **Keep it simple.** Onboarding emails don't have to be super short, but they should be easy to digest. Keep copy concise and include eye-catching visuals or gifs to guide readers through the email.

4. **Optimize for mobile.** Nowadays, the majority of emails (67%!) are opened on mobile. Create emails that render well on mobile. Knowing the ideal subject line length, button size, and CTA position is essential. Don't forget about the preview text!

5. **Segment your emails.** Not all user journeys are the same. Some will arrive via a social media promotion. Others will discover you from the app store. Some users will download your app, sign up, and immediately start poking around. Others will download and forget to ever open it. By segmenting new users and tailoring your welcome messages to their experience, you'll see up to 100.95% higher click-through rates and 18x more revenue.[43]

There are plenty of moving pieces to your onboarding series. Don't forget to experiment and split test different copies, timing, and creativity.

The Next Step

Many believe that moment—the signup—is when they've "won" the customer. But in reality, 40% to 60% of software users open an app once and never log in again. Using the BJ Fogg Behavior Model and increasing users' ability and motivation, and using behavior-based Prompts, you can keep new users engaged both inside and outside your product.

The final step in the EUREKA framework is to apply the changes we've discussed so far to your current user onboarding. Then, analyze the results.

And repeat.

Chapter 8 Summary

- The BJ Fogg Behavior Model is the key to unlocking behavior change and product adoption for new users. It emphasizes three elements that must converge simultaneously for a behavioral switch to occur:

  i. Motivation (M): The desire or willingness to do the new behavior.

  ii. Ability (A): The ease in doing the new behavior.

  iii. Prompt (P): The cue or trigger to do the new behavior.

- If users are falling off during the user onboarding, the BJ Fogg Behavior Model provides a framework to improve it:

  i. Is the new behavior as easy to do?

     o One useful concept to measure how easy (or hard) user onboarding is for new users is cognitive load—the mental effort required to learn new information. If the information exceeds the user's ability to handle it, it results in a cognitive overload.

     o With Straight-Line Onboarding in place from the previous chapter, you're already halfway there in making it easier.

     o You can take additional steps within your product to make for a remarkable first-time experience for new users that's both easy and effective.

1. Provide visual cues to guide them to the next onboarding step.

2. Show a helpful empty state.

3. Provide templates, cheat sheets, and other resources.

ii. Are users motivated to perform the behavior?

o Be careful in offering incentives for users to complete the onboarding process. External rewards might encourage users to complete the onboarding, but those users might not be interested in the product itself.

o Instead, use Product and Conversational Bumpers to increase a user's intrinsic motivations. There are a few ways to do this:

1. Speak to your users' desires.

2. Show them progress.

3. Welcome new users.

4. Celebrate their wins.

5. Use social proof.

iii. Are there prompts inside and outside your product to help users perform the desired behavior to complete the user onboarding?

o In the user onboarding experience, prompts are critical during two moments:

1. To help users achieve their desired outcome and experience the value of a product soon after signing up.

2. To help users continue to use a product until they adopt it into their life and workflow.

○ Successful and effective onboarding prompts have three qualities:

1. Prompts should be omnichannel, involving cohesive, thoughtful messaging across multiple channels that considers where users are in the onboarding journey.

2. Second, Prompts should be personalized and timely.

3. Third, Prompts should reiterate the value of your product.

○ At ProductLed, we use a three-step process to use Prompts in the onboarding process. You can apply this process to all types of Conversational Bumpers, such as SMS text messages, browser notifications, in-app messages, direct mail, and more.

1. Identify the key milestones in your Straight-Line Onboarding

2. Add behavior-based prompts based on the actions users take inside the product.

3. Fill in the details.

Action Items to Improve Your User Onboarding

- Review your Straight-Line Onboarding and look for opportunities to use Product and Conversational Bumpers to make it easier and increase user motivation.

- Use our three-step process to create a behavior-based onboarding communication plan.

Apply the Changes and Repeat

All life is an experiment. The more experiments you make, the better.

— Ralph Waldo Emerson

A few years ago, the designer and engineer Peter Skillman held a competition to build the tallest possible structure in 20 minutes with the following items:

- 20 pieces of uncooked spaghetti
- One yard of transparent tape
- One yard of string
- One standard-size marshmallow

The marshmallow had to be placed on top to win the competition, and the entire structure had to remain motionless for three seconds.

After running this challenge with more than 2,000 people from various backgrounds (from some of the top universities like Stanford, the University of California, and more to boot), Skillman was surprised by the results.

Business school students performed the worst. What was even more shocking was that the best performing group were not engineering prodigies or physics majors. They were kindergarteners.[44]

What happened?

The business students were talking and thinking strategically. They examined the materials. They brainstormed ideas, debated the best options, asked savvy questions, and homed in on the most promising ideas. It was professional, rational, and intelligent. The process resulted in a shared decision to pursue one strategy. Then, with five minutes left, they divided up the tasks and started to build.

The kindergartners took a different approach. Instead of strategizing, analyzing hypotheticals, debating, proposing, and asking questions, they simply start building. They rarely spoke to each other, and when they did, it was in short bursts, "Here! Now, here!"

By the time the 20 minutes were up, they had experimented with 8 to 10 different structures before landing on the most stable one.

In dozens of trials, kids built structures up to 26 inches tall, while business school students built structures less than 10 inches (on average). Kindergartners also beat out teams of lawyers (who built towers that averaged 15 inches), as well as teams of CEOs (22 inches).

Iterative Process > Big Launches

The lesson here: multiple iterations usually beat a commitment to the first idea and making it work. It's best to learn by doing.

This is an important principle to apply to user onboarding. From my experience, most teams do big launches to improve their user onboarding. Then, they iterate just once or twice a year. It's much better to analyze the results, reiterate and implement changes quickly than to overthink and strategize about it for months.

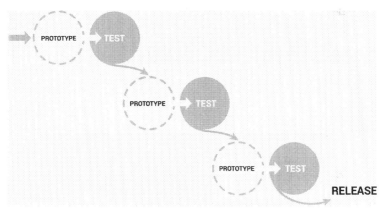

We're now at the final step of the EUREKA framework. It's time to apply changes to your onboarding experience. In this chapter, we'll discuss how to run rapid-fire experiments that will produce compounding wins.

The Growth Process

Companies that grow the fastest are also the ones that learn the quickest. They use this as a massive competitive advantage.

That's where our "Triple A" sprint comes in. It focuses on rapidly identifying problems, building solutions, and measuring impact. The process follows a one-month sprint cycle to identify and deliver an improvement to a product. It consists of three A's:

1. **Analyze**: Identify inputs that drive the outcomes you want for your business.
2. **Ask**: Answer these three questions:
   a. Where do you want to go?
   b. Which levers can you pull to achieve the desired outcome?
   c. Which inputs should you invest in?
3. **Act**: Choose an input and implement it.

Then, you go through the Triple A cycle again, considering any learnings from the previous iterations to future ones.

I use this process when working with ProductLed clients. But you can use any iterative growth process such as Sean Ellis' high-tempo four-step process,[45] Brian Balfour's six-step growth machine process[46], or Growth Tribe's G.R.O.W.S. process.[47]

You'll notice that most of the work you've completed for the EUREKA framework contributes to the Analyze and Ask steps of the Triple A process.

By now, the majority of the ideas to improve user onboarding should have emerged from the previous steps in the EUREKA framework. Those steps are focused on holistically analyzing your data and gathering insights as a cross-functional team.

Prioritizing Onboarding Improvements

From my experience, the problem in the growth process doesn't lie with Ideation but in the Prioritization of growth ideas. For that, I use the Action Priority Matrix:

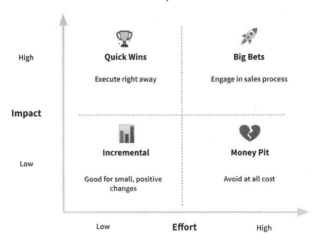

Here's what this means:

- High-impact, low-effort are low-hanging fruits and quick wins. Start with these ideas. This could be removing a field from your signup process.

- High-impact, high-effort could be big swings and transformational. These are major projects that require assessment and planning. This could be customizing the in-app onboarding experience based on the user's response on what they want to accomplish with your product.

- Low-impact, low-effort are momentum builders. These ideas are good as morale boosters but result in incremental improvements. This could be sending a behavior-based email to give users templates and inspirational content.

- Low-impact and high-effort ideas are ones to avoid.

Split Testing Growth Ideas

Ideally, you want to split test any onboarding changes. Let's say you want to validate that your Straight-Line Onboarding performs better than your current onboarding experience. You can send half of your new users through the new onboarding and the other half through your current process. After a few weeks, compare the week-to-week retention rate to determine if the retention curve has improved.

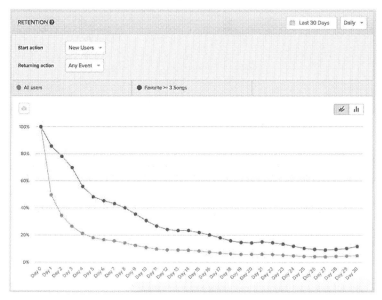

At this stage, it's critical to iterate quickly. If you're stuck at this step due to engineering bandwidth, consider tools like Appcues, Pendo, UserGuiding, and UserPilot to implement Product Bumpers. Userlist, Intercom or Drift can enact conversational bumpers.

Share Wins and Learnings

Another step that teams often miss is ensuring the learnings from each growth experiment are shared across the whole organization. Since changes in the user onboarding impact so many teams, it's really important to share the process, progress, and learnings with them.

Sharing with teams needs to become a habit.

Doing this will accomplish a few things. First, it excites your teammates (and the executive team) about onboarding. It's also a great way to create teamwide empathy to remind everyone that their work has a real impact on everyday lives. Finally, sharing the successes and impact of onboarding will ensure that you can continue to dedicate company resources to the project.

How you communicate this is entirely up to you, but here are a few things to try:

- An "Onboarding Wins" email that's sent out to the onboarding team and other coworkers who have expressed interest in the process.

- A dedicated Slack channel where you share test results and discuss upcoming tests.

- A slide deck in a shared folder (or in your company dashboards).

- An ongoing lunch-and-learn program.
- Monthly or quarterly meetings.

Beyond The Initial Onboarding

At this point, I want to stress once again that improving user onboarding is a continuous process. As your product evolves to the market it serves, the user onboarding experience must adapt to those product changes.

To that point, the process of onboarding users never ends.

As new users complete the initial onboarding and become regular users, your onboarding team can (and should) help them adopt new capabilities and use cases of the product.

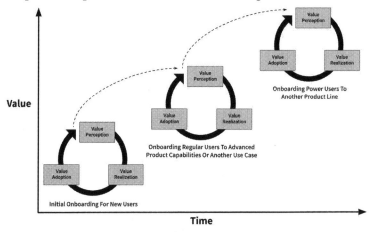

You can apply the same EUREKA process to various steps in the user journey. Here are some common places to consider:

- **Different entry points** to your product will require a different onboarding experience. The journey and knowledge of someone who signed up from an ad will likely be completely different from someone who signed up through a Google search or a webinar campaign.

- **Different Customer Jobs** will also require personalized onboarding.

- **Invited users** should be treated differently. You'll need to give them more information about why they're being invited and why they should use your product.

- **New UI and product changes** for existing users should be communicated thoughtfully. You'll find the most engaged users will be the most resistant to change. How can you implement the principles you've learned in the EUREKA framework to help them adopt those new changes?

Generally speaking, after the initial onboarding is completed, you can onboard users to go *deeper* or *wider* with your product.

Going Deeper

First, go deeper by educating new customers about advanced configurations and features to help them do a Customer Job more effectively.

For example, for sales executives who signed up for Calendly to meetings with prospects, the First Strike occurs when a prospect schedules a meeting using their Calendly link. For the next onboarding iteration, you could inform them about advanced features that would help them close more deals, such as:

- Embedding Calendly on a landing page.
- Sending SMS notifications to prospects so they don't miss meetings.
- Automatically distributing meetings to their team based on availability, priority, or equity.

- Integrating Facebook pixel code to the Calendly page to launch retargeting campaigns for those who viewed the Calendly page but didn't book a meeting.

Going Wider

The other option is to go *wider* by introducing solutions to different problems that your customers face.

For example, there are many reasons why people sign up for Hubspot:

- To generate leads with landing pages.
- Nurture and close leads with email workflows.
- Set up a company's website.
- Manage social media.
- Track the ROI of Facebook, Instagram, LinkedIn, and Google Ad campaigns with precision.
- Create and share links to book meetings with leads.
- Make, log, and record calls.
- Manage the sales team.

- Live chat with website visitors with a chatbot.

Let's say you know that a new customer signed up for Hubspot specifically to generate leads with landing pages. After achieving that objective, you can educate them on using social media to drive traffic to that landing page. If they have a sales team, you could also let them know about the benefits of subscribing to Hubspot Sales along with Hubspot Marketing.

Deeper or Wider?

So, what's the best option for your product after users complete the initial onboarding? It really depends on your audience. I'd suggest talking to them to explore what other problems they have that you can solve.

Are there problems that are an extension of a current one that your product solves, like with Calendly? Or are they adjacent to the ones your product solves like HubSpot? For your product, it could be both depending on the customer segments you serve.

Regardless, onboarding customers to additional capabilities and use cases of a product is critical for revenue expansion.

For example, with Intercom, a messaging platform that allows businesses to communicate with prospective and existing customers online, here's what a user journey could look like with them:

1. The initial onboarding cycle helps companies install live chat software on their website. This speeds up their acquisition time because they can respond to queries from prospects in real-time as visitors are surfing through pages.

2. Once users have started regularly using Intercom's live chat feature, the onboarding team helps users add smart

logic that directs conversations to relevant help articles or blog posts.

3. The next level helps companies automate conversations using chatbots.

With this example, the Intercom onboarding team assists users by providing more value over time. What's even more important is that they're encouraging users to upgrade their pricing tier: from $39 to $499 per month.

What's Next?

So far, I've covered the steps to improve your user onboarding without any assistance from anyone in your team. But sometimes it's best to have some help. In the next chapter, we'll look at how sales and high-touch support fit into the user onboarding experience.

Chapter 9 Summary

- When it comes to improving the user onboarding experience, it's much better to analyze the results, reiterate and implement changes quickly than to overthink and strategize about it for months.
- Use a prioritization framework to identify which onboarding improvements to test and implement first.
- Since changes in the user onboarding impact so many teams, it's really important to share the process, progress, and learnings with them.

  i. First, it excites your teammates (and the executive team) about onboarding.

  ii. It's also a great way to create teamwide empathy to remind everyone that their work has a real impact on everyday lives.

  iii. Sharing the successes and impact of onboarding will ensure that you can continue to dedicate company resources to the project.

- Generally speaking, after the initial onboarding is completed, you can onboard users to go deeper or wider with your product.

  i. Go deeper by educating new customers about advanced configurations and features to help them do a Customer Job more effectively.

  ii. Go wider by introducing solutions to different problems that your customers face.

Action Items to Improve Your User Onboarding

- Create a plan to ensure that the process, progress, and learnings in improving user onboarding are communicated with your entire organization. Here are some of the things I suggested in this chapter:

  o An "Onboarding Wins" email that's sent out to the onboarding team and other coworkers who have expressed interest in the process.

  o A dedicated Slack channel where you share test results and discuss upcoming tests.

  o A slide deck in a shared folder (or in your company dashboards).

  o An ongoing lunch-and-learn program.

  o Monthly or quarterly meetings.

Part III.
The Next Steps

CHAPTER 10:

Sales-Assisted User Onboarding

> *Approach each customer with the idea of helping him or her to solve a problem or achieve a goal, not of selling a product or service.*
>
> – Brian Tracy

"**W**hat do I need to do for you to try out a car today?" That sentence makes me cringe. It's the stereotypical sales tactic of the used car salesperson.

A few years ago, my wife and I were shopping for our first car together. We headed to a local car dealership. When we arrived, I made it clear to the sales rep that we didn't intend to buy anything that day. But the salesperson persuaded us into his office with free popcorn and mochaccinos (who can resist!). Then he showed us the best deals of the day. We sat in uncomfortable chairs for the entire afternoon while this fellow disappeared, emerging time and again with a new, lower price written on a sheet of paper.

After several rounds of this, we thanked him for his time and reminded him that we didn't intend to buy a car that day. We excused ourselves, with a piece of paper in hand, sealed with a promise that the price was good for the next few days.

Well, you can imagine what happened next.

A couple of days later, we caved. I phoned him up to tell him I was ready to buy and would be over shortly. I believed it would be an easy transaction, with my shiny new car waiting for me! No more need for haggling, or so I thought.

But when I got there, the same salesman told me the price was no longer available! Apparently, the manager who approved it made a mistake—at that price, the dealership would be losing money.

I left furious over the bait-and-switch and arrived at another dealership that offered the car for the price I wanted.

Chances are you've also run into a bad experience with a salesperson as well, whether it's buying a car, furniture, or even software. We often remember the bad experiences more than the good ones. But not every sales experience needs to be painful.

Good salespeople can add a ton of value to the buying process. When compared with a low-touch, product-led onboarding approach, sales-assisted onboarding can increase conversion rates by 3.5 times. Surprisingly, this can be true across all ranges of deal sizes for free trial B2B products.[48]

Sales Assistance Impact Evident at Every ACV
The Median Respondent with 15k-50k ACVs Converts Assisted Leads at 20%

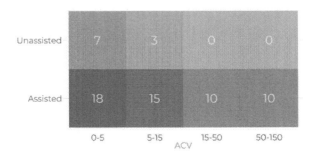

	0-5	5-15	15-50	50-150
Unassisted	7	3	0	0
Assisted	18	15	10	10

ACV

That's why most product-led companies eventually hire a sales team. For example, take a look at Slack, a classic example of a product-led company. If you think they don't have a sales team, you'd be wrong.

In 2019, 40% of Slack's revenue came from their sales team closing deals with larger organizations (companies making more than $100,000 in annual recurring revenue).[49] As a result, they experienced a 66% surge in marketing and sales expenses from 2018 to 2019.

	Year Ended January 31,		
	2017	2018	2019
	(In thousands, except per share data)		
Consolidated Statements of Operations Data:			
Revenue	$ 105,153	$ 220,544	$ 400,552
Cost of revenue[(1)]	15,517	26,364	51,301
Gross profit	89,636	194,180	349,251
Operating expenses:			
Research and development[(1)]	96,678	141,350	157,538
Sales and marketing[(1)]	104,006	140,188	233,191

As Slack proves, there's room to employ both a product-led and sales-led growth strategy to onboard new users. This approach is known as sales-assisted or hybrid onboarding.

In this chapter, we'll look at how the sales function can complement a PLG approach to user onboarding. My intention isn't to provide an in-depth focus on sales in a PLG model. I'm sure someone could write an entire book on that topic. My goal is to show you:

1. The differences between a sales-led, product-led, and hybrid onboarding.

2. How adding salespeople benefits the user onboarding process.

3. How the role of a salesperson differs in a PLG organization.

4. When and how a sales team should reach out to users.

Just a quick note—if you don't think you could ever benefit from a sales-assisted onboarding approach due to your product, target customer, or the market you serve, feel free to skip this chapter. Can you imagine Netflix hiring a bunch of salespeople to sell subscriptions? Me neither!

Sales-Led, Product-Led, and Sales-Assisted Onboarding

In a classic blog post titled, *The 5 ways to Build a $100 Million Business*, Christoph Janz explains the number of potential customers in your total addressable market. He describes how your business' annual contract value dictates your "hunting strategy," a.k.a. how you acquire, onboard, and retain new customers.[50]

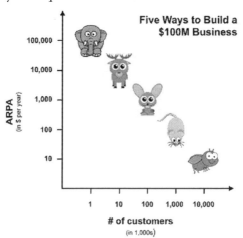

188 |

To build a $100 million business, you can hunt for:

- 1,000 "elephants," or enterprise customers who can each pay $100,000 or more per year.
- 10,000 "deers," or medium-sized companies that each pay $10k or more per year.
- 100,000 "rabbits," or small businesses that each pay $1k or more per year.
- One million "mice," or consumers who each pay $100 or more per year.
- Ten million "flies," or active users that you can monetize $10 or more per year each.

What you end up "hunting" for largely dictates whether you should adopt a sales-led, product-led, or sales-assisted approach to user onboarding. It also depends on the complexity of your buying process. To help visualize this, here are these two factors on a two-by-two matrix:

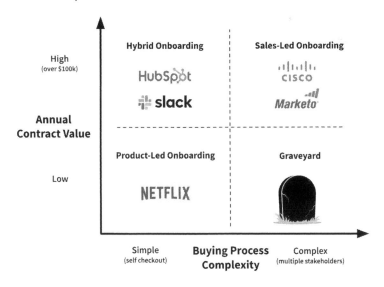

Here's a little rundown on when to use each approach:

- Suppose you have a high annual contract value (typically over $100,000) as well as a complex buying process with multiple stakeholders and a long sales cycle. In that case, consider onboarding new users using a high-touch, sales-led method. Cisco and Marketo are good examples of companies using this approach.

- If you offer a low annual contract value where users use a self-checkout process to purchase your product, then onboard new users with a low-touch, product-led process. Netflix is an excellent example of a company that employs a purely product-led onboarding approach.

- If the annual contract value ranges anywhere from $2,000 to over $100,000, then you should consider a mix between the two. In this case, the buying process complexity can vary from a simple self-checkout to complex multi-week sales check-ins.

   A company that transitioned from a sales-led to a hybrid onboarding approach is Hubspot. They moved down-market and released a freemium product for small and medium-sized businesses (SMB). Slack also transitioned from a product-led to a hybrid onboarding approach when they moved upmarket to sell to enterprise companies.

- If you have a low annual contract value and a complex buying process, then you'll be out of business sooner rather than later. Avoid this at all costs.

The key point here is that user onboarding doesn't have to fit into one box. You can think about it more like a continuum.

On one end is low-touch, product-led user onboarding. On the other is high-touch, sales-led onboarding. Where you end up on this continuum largely depends on your product, pricing, market, and buyer preferences.

From my experience, most successful B2B SaaS companies eventually adopt a sales-assisted onboarding strategy. For product-led businesses like Slack, Dropbox, and Drift, they end up hiring salespeople to onboard new users as they start pursuing larger deal sizes. For sales-led companies like HubSpot, Salesforce, and Vidyard, as they move downmarket, they shift their sales team to help new users find additional meaningful value with their product.

How Sales Can Complement Self-Serve Onboarding

"But we're product-led. Our product is self-serve. Visitors can sign up and purchase it without the need of any salespeople, right?"

I've heard this too many times to count.

This isn't always the case. Let me be clear—*being product-led doesn't automatically mean you're anti-sales.*

In this product-led era, we have a desire to move away from sleazy sales tactics, don't we? But good salespeople don't use unscrupulous methods to manipulate someone into buying something they don't need. When done correctly, they can add a ton of value to users in a PLG model. They make the product experience *better*.

In general, there are three primary reasons to add salespeople to self-serve onboarding:

1. Direct users to experience the value of your product

Sometimes even supposedly simple products have hidden hotspots that make it difficult for users to achieve their First Strike. This is where the "sales" team can be helpful. I place quotes around the word *sales* because this frequently looks more like support and customer success than sales. But the goal is the same: get the user to experience the value of your product, so they purchase it.

In a PLG model, salespeople act more like coaches. Going back to the analogy of the bowling alley, coaches guide users to hit more strikes consistently. Above all, coaches identify where users run into limitations and find a solution to overcome those challenges.

When free trial users get stuck installing the Appcues code snippet on their website, they don't talk to support on the phone. They speak to an account manager, who connects them with the right people to solve their issues.

2. Facilitate product penetration or expansion

This is the approach in the early days of Slack. Their sales team didn't send out cold emails that tend to pile up in an inbox: "Hi, if you need intra-organizational communication assistance, you should check out Slack."

Typically, one team within an organization first adopts Slack into their workflow. The role of the "Account Manager" (pssst... it's a salesperson) is to help get other teams within that organization to use Slack.

This is an example of the "land and expand" strategy. After you "land" a few users within a large company to sign up for a product, you "expand" by selling more seats and additional features for the organization. Often, this requires a sales team to make persistent, deep connections with high-level decision-makers. Salespeople work at the *account* level, not the *user* level.

3. Guide users in the buying process

For mid-size and enterprise companies, the buying process isn't always straightforward. For large companies, barriers often exist to purchase a product. This could include security audits, sign-offs from the procurement team, and requests for customized Service Level Agreements.

Whatever the reason, some users may *want* to talk to someone from your company. You could wait for them to schedule a meeting or book a call with prominent CTA's like "Contact Us" or "Contact Sales" on various pages on your site.

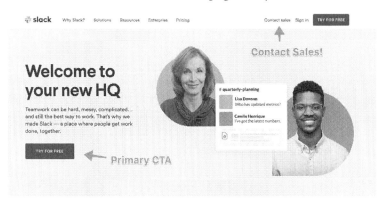

But smart product-led companies anticipate the needs of certain customers. They have sales teams armed and ready to reach out to these users before they run into barriers. Product-led onboarding is not about removing the sales function. It's about supporting new users. They don't badger, nag, or hound users with phone calls, emails, and text messages. Instead, they're consultative and helpful.

How The Role of a Salesperson Differs in a PLG Organization

Consultative selling (also called needs-based or solutions-based selling) is the key to how a sales function can complement a PLG approach. This approach shares many similarities with a product-led mindset. Both practices:

- Put the needs of users front and center throughout the customer journey, instead of running through a list of the latest bells and whistles, hoping that something grabs the prospect's attention.

- Maintain a clear focus on helping users achieve their desired outcome instead of trying to close a sale at any cost.

- Deliver a purchase experience that's more about being heard than about being sold to.

You're probably wondering, "How is this different from what good salespeople do in a sales-led organization?"

Indeed, PLG doesn't upend everything we know about sales. Many parts of the sales job remain the same. A deep understanding of the different stakeholders in the buying process remains important. There are still budget discussions to be had. And, of course, there is still a quota to hit.

But there are some subtle yet important differences in the sales process of a PLG model:

1. The salesperson shifts from chasing leads to coaching users

In a traditional sales model, the salesperson explains, shows, and demonstrates the value of the product or service. Prospects might not even have a clear understanding of their problem and your solution yet.

In a PLG model, users have already shown interest in a product. They've tried and tested out the product already. Hopefully, they've experienced the value of it. In this case, salespeople act more like coaches. In the analogy of the bowling alley, users are now familiar with the mechanics of bowling. They've achieved their First Strike and desired outcome.

Coaches guide users to hit more strikes consistently. Above all, coaches identify where users run into limitations and find a solution to overcome those challenges.

2. The salesperson needs to frame the product in different ways to different audiences.

In a PLG model, salespeople need to reframe the product's value and benefits for the end-user *and* the department heads and executives. This is a subtle but important difference. What end-users value might be different from what executives value.

To the end-user, they might be using the product to save time and perform their job better. For department heads and executives, they're likely looking at the expected ROI of the product.

Salespeople need the ability to pivot from one frame of reference to another quickly. They need to understand the pain points and opportunities for different stakeholders.

3. The salesperson has to leverage product engagement data in the sales process.

In a traditional sales model, salespeople usually qualify leads based on two factors:

- High-value interaction with marketing materials where leads become a Marketing Qualified Lead (MQL).

- Customer or company fit based on a checklist of the most common attributes someone needs to embody to become a successful customer for your offering. If they meet this requirement, leads become a Sales Qualified Lead (SQL).

After leads pass the qualification process, the sales process begins. It finishes when the prospect becomes a paying customer.

Soon after, the user onboarding process starts.

In a PLG model, an MQL could still exist. But since there's a lower barrier to product entry, the primary CTA for an MQL is the signup. Once users achieve meaningful value in the product, they become a Product Qualified Lead (PQL). Based on product engagement data and customer fit, the lead becomes an SQL, and the sales process kicks off.

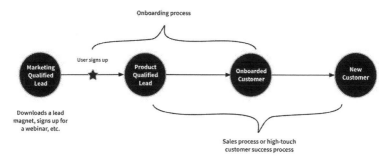

We've already briefly discussed PQLs in Chapter 6. Let's go into more detail in how a PQL fits into sales-assisted onboarding.

PQLs and SQLs in the Product-Led Sales

This one sounds obvious, but for a long time, the most qualified leads for a software product have never even used it before. PQLs are important to a consultative sales process. These are the users who are ready for a more in-depth conversation— they've already engaged with a product.

Traditional qualification criteria for PQLs include marketing activities (e.g. downloading an eBook, attending a webinar, etc.) or firmographic attributes (e.g. company size, industry, company, revenue, etc.) that imply an interest in the offering.

Nothing says "interested" like engaging with a product. So the more PQLs generated, the more consultative conversations a sales team can have.

Defining Your PQL

What makes a lead product qualified?

Generally speaking, a PQL is a measure of each new user's engagement with a product. This is a combination of:

- **Activation**: Has the user completed the Straight-Line Onboarding? If not, how far are they from completion?
- **Engagement**: How often are they using the product, especially the core features?

Here's how to find the answers to these questions for your SaaS business:

1. Set up a system to measure product engagement.
2. Define your PQL criteria.
3. Rank users by product engagement.

1. Set up a system to measure product engagement

Tracking product data is an integral part of qualifying leads based on product usage. Focus on the key milestones in your Straight-Line Onboarding. The goal is to know which users have not completed certain steps so the sales team can respond accordingly.

2. Define your PQL criteria

A PQL could involve multiple product engagement metrics including, but not limited to the following:

- The number of times the user has returned to the product.
- The number of other features the user has tested.
- How soon after signing up the user tries out additional features.

The exact criteria that go into defining a PQL will vary by company. But as a rule of thumb, a user who has completed the Straight-Line Onboarding and achieved their First Strike is a good indicator of a PQL.

As mentioned in Chapter 6, if you look at a continuum of user engagement—where one end indicates the moment a user signs up and the other end is the moment users achieve the Product Adoption Indicator—the PQL could manifest anyplace in the process.

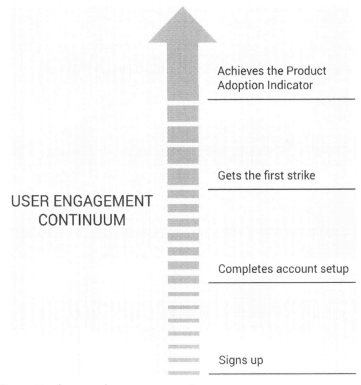

Achieves the Product Adoption Indicator

Gets the first strike

USER ENGAGEMENT CONTINUUM

Completes account setup

Signs up

3. Rank users by engagement

Once you've evaluated the product engagement metrics that make up a PQL, create a segment of users who have:

1. Completed the PQL criteria.
2. Not completed the PQL criteria.

Better yet, determine how far along users are in the PQL criteria, so you can rank them on how close they are to being qualified (a.k.a. a product engagement ranking model). This is how the sales team starts moving.

Doing this is not a simple task. Product events need to be based on how important they are. Then it's quite the job to keep up with each time an account uses important features over time.

If you're selling a B2B product, where multiple stakeholders in a company make the purchasing decision, the PQLs are accounts, not users.

The SQL in a Product-Led Sales Journey

Chances are, you don't want the sales team to reach out to every single PQL. Some might not be a good fit. Can you imagine Canva's sales team reaching out to a student who only wants to create graphics for her class presentation?

Focus your energy on PQLs who fit your ideal customer profile to make it worth the sales team's time and effort.

To find the ideal customer profile for your offering, create a list of specific attributes that an account needs to be successful with the product.

This could be:

- Company size
- Industry
- Annual revenue
- Role of contact
- Employee headcount — company-wide and within key departments
- Budget
- Geography

- Technology they use
- Size of their customer base
- Level of organizational or technological maturity

Next, find the common attributes of your best customers and create a list of them. Think of accounts that understood the product quickly and have now become raving fans. If they could, they'd give your product a Net Promoter Score of 11!

Steli Efti, Founder of Close.com, suggests that you find commonalities such as:[51]

- What's the size of the organization? (Measured in revenue, number of customers, number of employees, etc.)
- What's the size of the relevant department?
- Do certain job titles exist in the organization?
- Which industry or niche are they serving?
- How long have they already been in business?
- What's the number one reason that would prevent them from buying your solution?
- What's the number one reason that would make them decide to buy your solution?
- What makes your offer appealing to them?
- What goal do they want to achieve with your solution?
- How are they currently trying to achieve this goal?

Now, in a product-led sales journey, SQLs have two components:

1. They've engaged with your product enough that they've become a PQL.
2. They fit your ideal customer profile.

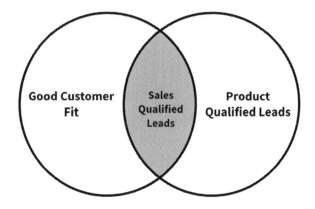

Once these are defined, leads who fit both criteria are ideal for sales-assisted onboarding.

If you map out product engagement on one axis of a four-by-four matrix and customer fit on another, you get the Product-Led Qualification Matrix created by Derek Skaletsky, CEO of Sherlock:[52]

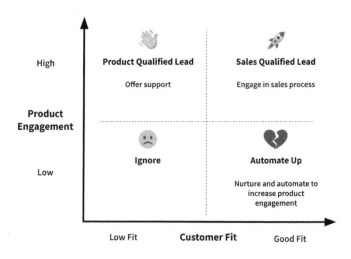

- Users who have high product engagement **and** are a good customer fit are the SQLs. Engage them in the sales process.

- PQLs are users who have high product engagement **and** are not a good customer fit. Offer support to them, but there isn't any need to engage them in the sales process unless they contact your team directly.
- Users who have low engagement **but** are good customer fit are known as the "heartbreakers." They're the dream customers, but they aren't engaging with the product. Nurture these users and offer support if they reach out.
- For users who have low engagement **and** are not a good customer fit, feel free to ignore them.

When and How Should Sales Reach Out To Users

It's a bit tricky to know when to get a salesperson involved once a lead becomes an SQL. An overly aggressive sales team could turn off prospects who only want to use the product and be left alone. Instead, the goal is to recreate the kind of experience we've come to expect from the Apple store—a friendly environment filled with experts who are ready to answer your questions, teach you about products, and help solve your problems.

With that in mind, sales outreach in a PLG model generally fits into two buckets: hand-raisers and proactive campaigns.

Hand-raisers are those who ask for help. Maybe they've filled out a form, asked a question using the in-app chat, requested a high-value feature, or sent you an email.

In these instances, sales reps should act more like a customer success team. Their role should be seen as a coach who works hand-in-hand with the customer to resolve blockers. They need to have a strong grasp of the product and customer use cases to cater to the distinct needs of different audiences. These team members should be motivated by understanding the product in a deep and meaningful way, not just crushing their quota.

On the other hand, proactive campaigns are manual or automated outreach to current users that generate demand for paid or higher-tier plans.

The focus is on high-value accounts that fit the ideal customer profile. The key is to find ideal moments in the user onboarding journey so that a sales outreach is welcomed:

- **After signing up:** sales can help users set up their accounts correctly and use the product to its full extent. This entails anything from implementing a complicated integration to guide the account through a proof-of-concept for a broad company-wide rollout.

- **Celebrate wins:** when users achieve something meaningful, such as completing their First Strike or setting up their account correctly, sales should show them some love and congratulate them. It's an opportunity for sales to offer additional support by guiding them to the next step or showing a demo of other helpful product features.

- **Going top-down:** once enough users sign up from one company, sales can initiate an outreach. The pitch should be tailored to the executive pain point. Ideally, lead with personalized insights based on the usage behavior of existing users from that account. This is what a communication tool for companies, Yammer, did to layer sales on top of their freemium offering. They prompted users to invite their coworkers. Once enough workers joined, their sales team would reach out. [53]

Whatever you do, make sure the sales team adds value to the product experience. You don't want them to add more friction than necessary. I've provided sales outreach email templates you can use in Appendix III.

What Comes Next?

My goal with this chapter was to show you how sales can *complement* your self-serve onboarding. When building out a sales-assisted or hybrid onboarding process, we've barely scratched the surface. Hiring a sales team, paying commissions for sales, and building product-led sales playbooks are all important factors to think about. For that, you can check out the following resources:

- *Predictable Revenue* by Aaron Ross and Marylou Tyler
- *The Sales Acceleration Formula* by Mark Roberge
- *Spin Selling* by Neil Rackham

And, of course, we'll be creating more content about product-led sales on productled.com.

Chapter 10 Summary

- Sales can complement self-serve onboarding by:
  i. Directing users to experience the value of your product.
  ii. Facilitating product penetration or expansion.
  iii. Guiding users in the buying process.

- The role of sales differs in a PLG organization:
    i. The salesperson shifts from chasing leads to coaching users.
    ii. The salesperson needs to frame the product in different ways to different audiences.
    iii. The salesperson has to leverage product engagement data in the sales process.
- The three steps to define your PQL:
    i. Set up a system to measure product engagement.
    ii. Define your PQL criteria.
    iii. Rank users by engagement.
- In a product-led sales journey, SQLs have two components:
    i. They've engaged with your product enough that they've become a PQL.
    ii. They fit your ideal customer profile.
- If you map it out on a four-by-four matrix with product engagement on one axis and customer fit on another, you get the Product-led Qualification Matrix:
    i. Users who have high product engagement and are a good customer fit are the SQLs. Engage them in the sales process.
    ii. PQLs are users who have high product engagement and are not a good customer fit. Offer support to them, but there isn't any need to engage them in the sales process unless they contact your team directly.

iii. Users who have low engagement but are good customer fit are known as the "heartbreakers." They're the dream customers, but they aren't engaging with the product. Nurture these users and offer support if they reach out.

iv. For users who have low engagement and are not a good customer fit, feel free to ignore them.

  o For high-value accounts, find ideal moments in the user onboarding journey so that a sales outreach is welcomed:

v. After signing up: sales can help users set up their accounts correctly and use the product to its full extent.

vi. Celebrate wins: when users achieve something meaningful, such as completing their First Strike or setting up their account correctly, sales should show them some love and congratulate them.

vii. Going top-down: once enough users sign up from one company, sales can initiate an outreach.

Action Items to Improve Your User Onboarding

- Work with your onboarding team to define your PQL.
- If it's appropriate for your business, start building a sales process to complement your product-led onboarding process. Identify ideal moments in your Straight-Line Onboarding for a sales outreach.

CHAPTER 11:

Where Do We Go From Here?

Retention is the most important thing for growth.

    - Alex Shultz, VP Analytics and CMO at Facebook

G reat businesses are built on high customer retention. It's not about everyone hearing about a product—it's about those who use it successfully. A great onboarding experience is a foundation for high customer retention.

I had to learn this the hard way while consulting for a SaaS company a few years ago.

Maybe you can relate?

My team and I were spending thousands of dollars on ads and taking hours (and even weeks!) to build content for SEO.

We were getting a ton of signups, which was awesome.

But very few signups converted into paying customers. (So few that it was downright embarrassing.)

I started digging into the data and realized that new users were getting stuck… but where?

In the onboarding!

That's when I immediately started to optimize it as best I could. And, surprise, surprise, as soon as I was done, we saw a HUGE uplift in free users turning into paying customers. Not only that, I realized that users who completed the user onboarding process stuck around much longer than those who didn't.

I had to know if I could carry out the same optimization process for other companies and achieve the same excellent results. That's when I started working with Wes Bush at ProductLed to see if this was a repeatable framework.

Sure enough, it was!

One of our clients doubled their trial-to-paid conversion rate. This drove a 315% increase in MRR in six months, just by removing one step in their user onboarding!

It was clear Wes and I were onto something. And after seeing the results from our techniques time and again, I started documenting them so that I could share our discovery with others one day.

That's how the EUREKA framework was born:

1. **Establish your onboarding team:** To deliver an effective, immersive, and seamless onboarding experience for new users, your approach needs to be collaborative across functions and departments. Onboarding can't just be quilted together from the work of different departments. It must be holistic. If it's not, users receive a fractured experience.

2. **Understand your user's desired outcomes:** The best way to get users to perceive, realize, and adopt the value of a product is to figure out the reason they signed up in the first place. Particularly, you need to define what *value* means to your users.

3. **Refine your onboarding success milestones:** Your team needs to have a clear picture of what it means to successfully onboard new users.

4. **Evaluate and optimize your onboarding path:** To minimize the time it takes for new users to experience a product's value, you have to map out your user's journey and determine which steps should be delayed or eliminated.

5. **Keep new users engaged:** To help guide new users to experience your product's value, consider using triggers inside and outside your product. These could include product tours, welcome messages, progress bars for in-app triggers and onboarding emails, SMS and app notifications.

6. **Apply the changes and repeat:** User onboarding is a continuous process, and you need to continue to iterate on the onboarding experience.

Congratulations! You've made it through the EUREKA framework to improve your user onboarding.

One final tip: the most successful teams don't look at improving their onboarding as a one-time action item. It's a cyclical process that becomes vital to the success of your product. That's why the EUREKA framework must become part of your product design and development process.

When the onboarding experience is seamless, it feels like magic. It's hard to revert to the way tasks used to get done. Get user onboarding right, and new users experience a "Eureka!" moment and embrace the product into their lives.

All thanks to a better onboarding experience!

Thanks for Reading Product-Led Onboarding!

By now, you know the importance of user onboarding to the growth of a company. You've also learned a step-by-step framework to onboard more new users and turn them into lifelong customers. But, for every one person, there are thousands who still waste a ton of time and resources on acquiring more users, even with a low converting user onboarding experience.

If you found this book helpful, I encourage you to share it with a friend and colleague. It would also mean so much to me if you would review this book online. Your review goes a long way toward encouraging other people to read *Product-Led Onboarding*, and I'd consider it a *huge personal favor*.

Thank you in advance! Please go to ProductLedOnboarding.com/review

Onwards together,

Ramli John

P.S. If you have any questions or want to share how you're going to implement the EUREKA framework to your product-led onboarding, send me an email at ramli@productled.com or message me on Twitter (@RamliJohn), LinkedIn (https://linkedin.com/in/ramlijohn), or the PLG Slack Community (https://productled.com/slack). I'd love to hear from you!

Acknowledgments

This book's purpose is to serve you—the reader. You're in the trenches working to grow a business, whether you're in a sales, marketing, customer success, growth, or design team. This book's job is to give you the knowledge and framework I wish I had while working with clients to improve their user onboarding experience.

If you found this book valuable, that's because a wide range of people contributed their time and provided me encouragement and support. Writing a book is both joyful and painful at the same time. There were many times during the last eight months when I wanted to give up. On top of that, writing doesn't come naturally for me; I have a math degree, and English is my second language. So without the support, encouragement, and feedback from the folks below, Product-Led Onboarding would not have been possible.

First and foremost, I want to thank Wes Bush for his trust, guidance, and encouragement. He was the first one to recognize the possibilities of this book well before anyone else. Where others saw a jumble of notes and ideas, he saw what it could be. Wes, I'll always be thankful for your counsel and friendship.

To the team at ProductLed, thank you. To Laura Kluz, our Head of Content and book editor, you added life and humor to my words. This book wouldn't be as great as it is without you. To Gretchen Duhaime, our Director of Operations, you were the magician that pulled strings behind the scenes that made the book launch happen. You are truly the glue that holds our team together.

To the ProductLed community and alumni of the Product-Growth Certification Programs, thank you for being so engaged and providing very early feedback on the materials of this book. You didn't know it then, but I was testing out the concepts that would later become this book. So, for trusting me in the process, thank you.

To all the beta readers, thank you for taking the time to give me your thoughts on the book: Abdullah Kamel, Adam Haas, Alexander Rodny, Allan Yu, Alvaro Barbosa, Amanda Williams, Andy Dent, Anne Susalski, Anthony Franklin, Antonio Gomes, Arqum Younus, Aryna Dashkovskaya, Ben Hong, Bohdan Drozdov, Bruno Cambraia Nunes, Carl Winans, Carla Ancora, Caroline Bagby, Chris Dietrich, Christos Passas, Clarence Wong, David Espinel, David Isaac, David Welch, Deepa Buddhavarapu, Devashish Datt Mamgain, Doug Claffey, Eric Putnam, Ertugrul Cavusoglu, Eugene Sega, Gabor Kiss, Giseli Barbosa Anversa, Gratsiela Zhalova, Harpreet Bambra, Hugo Manuel Antunes Alves, Ian Booth, Jacqui Jones, Jai Wright, Janice Sousa, Jeanette Dorazio, Jennifer Rohleder, Jimmy Louchart, Jon Johnson, Kane Sivesind, Kate DeGroot, Kedar

Parikh, Kris Sharma, Leonor Reis, Ligia Braga, Mahmoud Hashim, Maria De Souza, Mark Bradley, Martin Lasarga De Maria, Marwan Dajani, Michael Melo, Nadav Lotan, Natalia Jaworska, Nate Smoyer, Netali Jakubovitz, Nicki Friis, Oana Andruc, Pawel Sokolowski, Priya Badger, Rachel Lanham, Rahul Jain, Reuben Piryatinsky, Ritesh Kumar, Rob Helderman, Ronak Ganatra, Ryan Quiel, Seyma Dogan, Shannon Ahmed, Simon Balz, Søren Fuhr, Stefanie Dolhausen, Stella Canivenc, Stephen Jeske, Steve Copley, Tarin Poddar, Taylor Jones, Troy Winfrey, Varun Sidhu, Wei Wang, Wiehan Britz, Will Royall, and Zoe Pollard, and Michaela Heigl.

Out of all the beta readers, five stood out as ones that made major contributions to the book:

- Anuj Adhiya—Your honesty is brutal and refreshing. Thank you for pointing out major gaps in the book. I know that it came from a place of love and respect. Thank you for your time; I know how valuable it is, knowing how busy you are working with several startups. Cheers, mate!

- Amanda Natividad—Not only was your feedback useful in making my writing clearer, but you also did it in such a way that made me laugh along the way. Your positivity and thoughtfulness really shined through in the comments you left. Thank you!

- Josh Ho—Thank you for your detailed review of the book. I removed a whole chapter because of it! I can't imagine what this book would have been like without you. And, of course, you gave a testimonial. I appreciate it!

- Emanuel Petrescu—Thank you for being my earliest supporter, all the way back to when I started my first podcast, Growth Marketing Today. You were the first one to give me feedback on this book.
- Bohdan Drozdov—You found a major miscalculation in two of the graphs in Chapter 6. Thank you for taking the time to comb through the data and help me find this error before it went live.

To Sean Ellis, Ethan Garr, Nir Eyal, Claire Suellentrop, Andrew Capland, Jane Portman, Eric Keating, Tara Robertson, Corey Haines, Katelyn Bourgoin, Anuj Adhiya, Anna Talerico, Brennan McEachran, Amanda Natividad, Josh Ho, Maja Voje, Danny Villareal, Adrienne Barnes, Ronak Ganatra, Emily Lonetto, and Josh Garofalo—thank you for reading the draft and trusting me enough to give a testimonial for the book.

On a personal level, I want to thank my parents, Ramon and Lina. You helped shape me to become who I am and instilled values that are firmly rooted in our faith. Whenever I had big goals, instead of telling me to have more realistic dreams, you fanned the flame and told me I could be whomever I wanted to become. Thank you for telling me that you love me and you're proud of me. I'm privileged to have parents whom I don't feel like I have to earn their respect and love.

For anyone who is still reading this, I got my name "Ramli" from the first part of "Ramon" and "Lina." Ram-Li... get it? :-)

Finally, to my forever bride, Joanna Ruth. You are my sunlight and God's favor in my life. You saw me at my lowest while writing this book, smacking my head on the table wondering if I made a mistake in writing this book. I laughed, cried, and paced back-and-forth like a mad man. You encouraged me and served as a sounding board during the ups and downs of the writing process. Your endless affection leaves me forever in your debt; I'm wondering how I ever got so lucky. Here's to many more years together!

Suggested User Onboarding Resources and Tools

That's the end of this book. But, there are a ton of other available resources and tools to help you improve a product's user onboarding. Here are some that I personally recommend.

Communities

ProductLed.com/community — Join our community of product-led growth enthusiasts to meet world-class PLG practitioners that you can learn from.

ForgetTheFunnel.com — A community of over 5k SaaS marketing, growth and product leaders to learn a systematic customer-led approach.

SwipeFiles.com — A community for marketers and entrepreneurs to brainstorm marketing and product challenges and get your questions answered.

Content

Productled.com/blog — You can find the latest ProductLed articles, videos, and guides here.

onboardingteardowns.com — I show how popular product-led businesses onboard new users.

useronboard.com — Samuel Hulick, a UX strategy consultant, is one of the user onboarding leaders. His onboarding teardowns and articles are one of the best!

DeliveringValue.co — Andrew Capland, Head of Growth at Postscript (previously at Wistia), shares his growth process, which is critical for improving user onboarding.

BreakoutGrowth.net — A blog and podcast by Sean Ellis and Ethan Garr. You'll find here practical, actionable content and learnings to put principles of sustainable growth into motion.

openviewpartners.com/blog — Get insights, actionable advice, and founder interviews aimed at helping you grow your product-led company.

bit.ly/andrewchen-magic-number — Andrew Chen, General Partner at Andreessen Horowitz (a Silicon Valley venture capital firm), provides a guide to help you find insights like Facebook's "7 friends in 10 days."

Books

Hooked by Nir Eyal — Get users hooked on your product using the simple, but powerful framework from this book.

Hacking Growth by Sean Ellis and Morgan Growth — Learn the growth playbook used by the fastest growing companies in Silicon Valley and beyond.

Tiny Habits by BJ Fogg — A habit expert from Stanford University, Dr. Fogg breaks down his framework for helping people build positive habits and let go of old ones.

Obviously Awesome by April Dunford — You can't design a great user onboarding experience without first nailing your product positioning. April reveals her 10-step positioning framework.

Don't Make Me Think by Steve Krug — I consider this the ultimate guide to help you understand the principles of intuitive navigation and information design. Many product designers call this the bible of usability design.

Lean Analytics by Alistair Croll and Benjamin Yoskovitz — The core idea behind *Lean Analytics* is this: by knowing the kind of business you are, and the stage you're at, you can track and optimize the One Metric That Matters to your startup right now.

Never Lose a Customer Again by Joey Coleman — This is my favorite book on designing a customer experience that results in increased customer loyalty and retention. Coleman identifies eight distinct emotional phases customers go through in the 100 days following a purchase.

Tools

Appcues.com, Pendo.io, TryChameleon.com, Userpilot.com, Userguiding.com, and WalkMe.com — These are some of the best in-app user engagement platforms. They're useful for building product tours, checklists, welcome messages, and more.

SparkToro.com — An audience research tool that helps you discover any audience's sources of influence: who and what they follow, visit, read, watch and listen to.

ReferralRock.com — Once new users are onboarded to your product, one of the things you want to encourage them to do is to refer it to their friends and colleagues. You can use ReferralRock to incentivize them to do so using an on-brand sharing experience that generates more referrals.

ActiveCampaign.com, Intercom.com, Userlist.com — These are some of the best behavior-based customer messaging tools for user onboarding.

Services

HeyElevate.com — Founded by Georgiana Laudi (former VP Marketing at Unbounce) and Claire Suellentrope (former Head of Marketing at Calendly), Elevate helps SaaS companies identify and act on high ROI opportunities, including user on-boarding. They've worked with companies such as FullStory, Appcues, Sprout Social, and more.

CustomerCamp.com — Customer Camp is a training and research firm that helps growth-ready product teams to get inside their customer's heads so they can market smarter.

SimpleCircle.co, Useronboard.com, and TheProductOn-boarders.com — These are freelancers or agencies that specialize in helping tech companies improve their user onboarding experiences.

About the Authors

Ramli John is the Managing Director at ProductLed, where he works with companies such as Mixpanel, Microsoft, Ubisoft, and more to accelerate their growth. An educator at heart, he has helped train hundreds of the world's fastest-growing product-led companies to level up their user onboarding experience to turn more users into lifelong customers.

Ramli holds a Bachelor of Mathematics Degree from the University of Waterloo and an MBA from Richard Ivey School of Business. He's a seasoned podcast host, first with the Growth Marketing Today show and now with the Product-Led Podcast, interviewing top product and marketing leaders such as Sean Ellis, April Dunford, and Hiten Shah.

Wes Bush is the founder and CEO of ProductLed. He is the bestselling author of *Product-Led Growth: How To Build a Product That Sells Itself* and is one of the most sought-after product experts in the world. After working for some of the world's fastest-growing companies in the world, today he trains teams around the globe on how to turn their product into a powerful growth engine.

Wes holds a Bachelor's Degree in Global Business and Digital Arts from the University of Waterloo. A respected business consultant, Wes understands that flashy marketing and hard sales can't replace the value a customer receives from an exceptional product.

Don't miss the other book from the ProductLed Library: *Product-Led Growth*

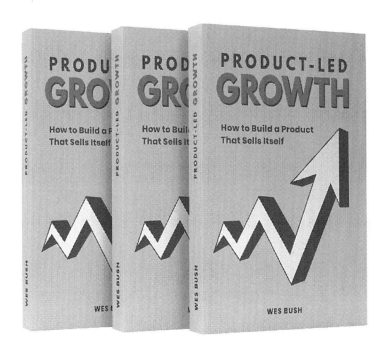

Discover the fundamentals of Product-Led Growth and how you can turn your product into a growth engine, widen your funnel, and dominate your market while cutting your customer acquisition costs.

Available now on Amazon, Audible, Barnes & Noble, or ProductLedBook.com

Appendix

Appendix I:
Jobs-to-be-Done User Interviews

Here are the five steps to doing Jobs-to-be-Done interviews:

Step 1: Select and Contact Interviews Subjects

The first step is to choose who you want to talk to. There are five types of people you interview:

1. New users who just signed up
2. Churned customers
3. Shoppers – people who are actively evaluating your product
4. Active customers
5. Inactive customers

The best place to start is to interview your best-ft customers. These are customers who understood your product quickly, bought it without hesitation, and referred you to other companies or people. Try to understand what they love about your product and why they decided to switch to it in the first place.

You also want to interview inactive users, along with churned customers, to find out if there are gaps with your product positioning or onboarding messaging: Did you over-promise and underdeliver? Did they sign up thinking your product could solve a problem that it really couldn't?

Interviewing these folks might be challenging. They might be skeptical, thinking that you're trying to win them back. You want to make it clear that you're doing this for research purposes. You could also offer an incentive, whether that's a $50 Amazon gift card or some company swag.

Once you've compiled a list of 10 to 20 people, reach out. Here's a sample:

Subject: Share your experience and get **[incentive]**

*Hey **[NAME]**,*

*I'm **[my name]**, and I'm part of the **[my company]** team.*

I'm doing research to better understand how you use our product in a short 30-minute call.

*We want to better understand our users. After our chat, I'll take what I've learned and share it with my team so we can improve **[your product]**.*

*It'd be an easy 30-minute chat, and we'll give you **[incentive]** for your time.*

*If so, feel free to choose the time that works best for you here **[insert link to your scheduling tool]**.*

Looking forward to our chat.

Thanks,

[YOUR NAME]

You might be surprised how willing people are to talk about their experiences. Especially your most active customers; they have a lot to share. Put yourself in their shoes – imagine if someone from a product you're a fan of asks if they can talk for some feedback. Hell yeah!

You want to set their expectations. Make sure they know how long an interview is going to take. I usually start by asking for 30 minutes. Anything less means you'll likely rush through questions and not reach as deep.

One final tip before you send out interview invitations. Send out your emails in batches. First, this will help you spread out interviews over a few weeks. Second, it'll let you do small tweaks to your invite and try different incentives if you're getting low response rates.

Step 2: Prepare a Jobs-to-be-Done interview script

Once you have a few interviews booked, it's time to prepare your script.

Talking to a stranger can be weird. So take a few minutes at the start of the interview to let them know there are no right or wrong answers and you just want to hear what they think.

This is also the moment where you should ask if they are OK with being recorded. The majority of people won't mind. (I've not had anyone say they don't want to be recorded.)

By preparing in advance and drafting this opening, you won't overthink what to say, and instead, you can focus on seeming friendly and inviting.

To get a full picture of their experience, here is a list of questions you can ask:

The first thought / the functional job

- When did you first realize you needed something to solve [your problem]?
- What were you doing, or trying to do, when this happened?
- Before you began [using the current solution], how did you solve these same problems in the past?
- When did you realize the old way wasn't working?
- When were you forced to make a change?
- Was there a deadline or specific event you needed to be ready for?
- What alternatives did you consider before using [the solution]?
- What was good or bad about each of those?
- What was the hardest part of figuring out what solution to use?
- Was there any point where you got stuck?
- With [the solution], what can you do that you couldn't do before?

- Did you alone make this decision to change, or was someone else involved?
- What other changes did you have to make to integrate [the solution] into your life?

Emotional and social jobs

- Tell me about how you looked for a product to solve your problem.
- What job are you ultimately trying to get done?
- Were you able to accomplish this with [your product]? What kind of solutions did you try? Or not try? Why or why not?
- Did you ask anyone else what they thought about the purchase you were about to make?
- What was the conversation like when you talked about purchasing the product with your [friend/colleague/boss/parents]?
- Before you purchased it, did you imagine what using the product would be like? Where were you when you were thinking this?
- Did you have any anxiety about the purchase? Did you hear something about the product that made you nervous? What was it? Why did it make you nervous?
- How do you use the product you've purchased?
  - Are there features you use all the time? How?
  - Are there features you never use? Why not?
  - What's something you wish [your product] could do?

One tip before you interview your users: think of your script as guidelines. It's nice to have it, but it's also important to know when to deviate from it. If you feel there's something more to an answer, stay there, and dig deeper with follow-up questions. Be curious, and don't stick to your script in a robotic manner.

Step 3: Conduct the interview

It's time to conduct the interview. Once you've asked for permission to record the call for research purposes... hit record. I've forgotten to hit that button once or twice. It's unfortunate because recording interviews frees you up so you don't have to take very detailed notes.

In terms of tools, I use Zoom to do the calls. But if you prefer doing phone interviews, you can try Uberconference.com.

Step 4: Transcribe and Organize Interview Scripts

Once you have a recording, transcribe it using services like Rev.com or Otter.ai. Then, read through the transcript and highlight meaningful portions of the interview. You want to be looking for six main insights:

1. **Struggling moments**: What was the problem or struggle that caused the person to start seeking a new solution? For example, "I'm trying to improve the number of leads I generate each month, but I'm not sure how to set up campaigns on Facebook..."

2. **Motivations**: What was the person trying to accomplish with the new solution? For example, "I want to figure out how to build out a Facebook lead funnel to automate the whole process of lead generation..."

3. **Driving forces**: What were the emotions the person felt that caused them to seek a new solution instead of continuing to do things the way they already are? For example, "I'm frustrated that I haven't hit my lead gen goal in the last couple of months."

4. **Perceived value:** How did the person envision life being better once they have a new solution? For example, "I was hoping to find an easy, scalable way to convert & retain more paying customers."

5. **Experienced value:** What was the person's life like after they've successfully used your product? If they churned from your product, what were they disappointed with? For example, "I'm now able to easily convert and retain more paying customers without hand-holding each one."

6. **Solutions considered:** What were other solutions they considered? What criteria did they use to evaluate different solutions and choose the right one for them?

It can get messy with all the notes. You can use the customer data spreadsheet that we use at ProductLed for our clients found at productled.com/user-interviews.

Step 5: Gather the insights and implement them

Once you're done with the interviews and you've highlighted key quotes from the transcripts, start coding your data to classify your findings.

So… when are you done with interviews? When you stop hearing new data from new interviewees. If you get 2–3 interviews where 80% of the information is stuff you've already heard, chances are you don't need it anymore. Still, you don't want to have fewer than 15-ish calls. And remember – the more concrete your interview criteria are, the fewer interviews you'll need to conduct.

You can group your insights into "themes" or key phrases. For example, if an insight reads, "It was more fun than expected," and another is, "It's fun to watch because of the graphics and the video," both of these can be categorized as "Enjoyable."

Then you want to add up all the themes to see which themes recur most often.

Remember, this is qualitative research. And as such, you're not focused on crunching the numbers. They are here to give you a relative understanding of what matters to the majority of your customers.

Appendix III: Product Bumpers

This is an excerpt of Chapter 13 from
Product-Led Growth by Wes Bush.

Product bumpers help users experience meaningful value in the product. Out of the two bumpers, product bumpers are arguably the most important. That's because if you help people accomplish something meaningful in their life with your product, they'll come back on their own.

That's not to say that conversational bumpers aren't useful—they just play a different role. For instance, if someone signs up but never touches foot in your product, the best product bumper in the world won't help you.

Given the importance of product bumpers, I want you to identify one or two that can guide your users to the promised land. Maybe there's an area in your onboarding that could benefit from a progress bar or checklist. Who knows?!

Here are the main product bumpers I'll break down:

1. Welcome Messages
2. Product Tours

3. Progress Bars
4. Checklists
5. Onboarding Tooltips
6. Empty States

1.   Welcome Messages

If you knock on a door to a friend's house, what kind of response would you expect? Would your friend welcome you? Or would they not say a single word, letting you walk around their house and eat the food in the fridge?

The second scenario sounds weird. Friends say hello to friends. But in user onboarding, companies often forget to welcome guests who sign up for a product. It's a "help yourself to the kitchen" mentality. As a user, it can feel odd. We have an innate desire to feel welcomed.

In this example by ConnectHero, they showcase a message from the CEO that personally welcomes the user to the product.

ConnectHero

Welcome, Jennifer!

My name is Matt Brown, founder of ConnectHero, and I'm so glad to see you here! Since we founded the company in 2010, we've been able to help 100's of incredible companies like WeatherTech, Dell, and Nike save countless hours responding to customer messages. Now, I can't wait to help your ecommerce businesses!

Matt Brown
CEO & Founder of ConnectHero

Next →

• • • • • • •

The message explains why the founder created the product and restates the value proposition. Welcome messages can also increase a user's motivation for using the product by clearly explaining the value and building suspense.

Key Takeaways:

1. Welcome messages are your opportunity to greet new users and make them feel invited—you are the host, after all.

2. In addition to saying hello, use them as an opportunity to restate your value proposition and increase users' motivation before they use the product.

3. Welcome messages can also set expectations for what users will experience with your product.

Now that we've welcomed new users, it's time to help them set up their account—fast.

2. Product Tours

Product tours are the ultimate product bumper. They eliminate distractions and give you only a few important options. In my experience, I reserve product tours for the most important green-light items in your straight line. I recommend using only three to five steps in your product tour.

As you can see below, ConnectHero uses a product tour to help us select which help desk solution we'd like to integrate:

ConnectHero

Choose Your Help Desk

zendesk	desk	freshdesk	Help Scout	gorgias
Zendesk	Desk.com	Freshdesk	Help Scout	Gorgias

Don't see your help desk or have one yet? Learn more.

With this approach, your response can trigger a different straight-line onboarding track—one that's specific to your desired outcome (e.g., forwarding your Amazon and eBay messages to Zendesk).

If you have a multi-product business, using a product tour at the beginning of your onboarding can be a gamechanger. You catapult people into the areas of the product that they care most about.

If you have a simple consumer application, you might be able to get away without using a product tour. But if you have a complex product with features that accomplish different tasks, a product tour is a must.

I recommend using a "focus mode" that hides background elements to minimize the initial number of choices. Such product tours are extremely effective because they leverage Hick's Law (decision time increases with every additional choice) and the Paradox of Choice (more choices make people less likely to choose).

By eliminating the number of decisions a new user has to make, you increase the likelihood that they will make the right decision. When structuring your product tour, don't reinvent the wheel. Include some of the required green steps in your straight line to help your product deliver on its value faster.

Key Takeaways:

1. Product tours should ask users what they're trying to accomplish in the product.
2. Product tours should cover important step(s) that set users up for success with the product.
3. High-performing product tours often use a "focus mode" that strips away unnecessary elements, like the navigation bar, until the user completes the product tour.
4. Product tours are typically between three and five steps.

All in all, product tours are one of the most effective ways to bump users toward experiencing meaningful value in the product. Typically, this kind of forceful bump is best deployed at the beginning of a user journey; however, as the user progresses along your straight line, you might want to use a more gentle bump, such as progress bars.

3.   Progress Bars

Progress bars indicate how far a user has come and how far they need to go. When running a marathon, I look forward to seeing the markers for each kilometer—they remind me of how far I've run and how far I have to go.

At first, it can be demotivating to see that you've run only 1 out of 42 kilometers. However, once you get close to the 30-kilometer mark, your motivation goes up. You push yourself harder until you cross the finish line.

The same principle holds true for user onboarding. Humans are addicted to progress and will work hard to finish something once they think it's achievable. One caveat: Goals need to seem realistic. Just think of how demoralizing it would be to sign up for an account only to see a progress bar with "0 out of 99" steps completed.

Break down goals to make them achievable. Think about a marathon. Forty-two kilometers sounds intimidating, but dividing it into nine 5-kilometer races helps you feel like you're constantly making progress.

Progress bars can come in many shapes and sizes. <u>According to Formisimo</u>, here are the most common progress bars:

If we were to put what we just learned into action, we could simply add a progress bar to our product tour for ConnectHero. Voila!

ConnectHero

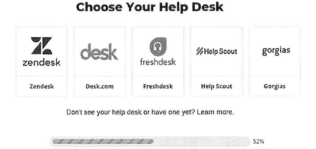

Now, we're setting an expectation for how many steps are ahead for our users. This reassures them that the onboarding process won't take long, and that they're only a few steps from completion. As a result, users are more likely to stick around.

Key Takeaway:

- Effective progress bars start with a substantial percentage of the bar already filled. This helps users feel like they're already underway instead of starting from scratch, and it increases the desire to complete the task.

After the initial setup is complete—and progress bars are filled—what's next? You often need to give specific instructions. Onboarding checklists are a great way to go.

4. Onboarding Checklists

Checklists break down big tasks into bite-sized ones. For ConnectHero, we could use an onboarding checklist to help users set up their account:

ConnectHero

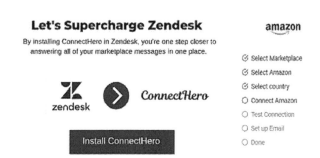

But checklists alone can take you only so far. If you want to get the most out of your onboarding checklists, have them partly filled out by the time the user sees them. This simple tactic employs the "<u>endowed progress effect</u>"—people who think they're close to completing something are more likely to see it through.

In addition to giving users an overview of how to set up their account, checklists simultaneously increase user motivation because users know how many steps it takes. For best results, I recommend having between three and five checklist items for a new user to complete.

According to <u>Zapier</u>, onboarding checklists also work well because of the <u>Zeigarnik Effect</u>, our tendency to think about incomplete tasks more than completed ones. Not finishing a task nags at us. Researchers call this "task tension." Only completing the task can relieve it.

It's why cliffhangers are effective in movies and television. It's why crossing off an item on your to-do list feels satisfying. It's also why seeing 59 unread Facebook Messages might freak you out.

Key Takeaways:

1. Checklists can motivate new users to complete crucial setup tasks.

2. Checklists can turn complex, multi-step processes—such as scheduling a month of social media content—into simple, achievable tasks.

3. Onboarding checklists employ the Endowed Progress and Zeigarnik Effect.

If there are specific actions that users need to complete, onboarding is an effective way to motivate users. However, sometimes you also need to show users how to do something. That's where onboarding tooltips come in.

5. Onboarding Tooltips

Onboarding tooltips help users learn how to use a product. They can reduce the burden on support and scale usability. Here are the main ways you can use hotspots and action-driven tooltips:

1. Show first-time users how to use the product.

2. Offer helpful tips to new users. Think of this like coaching.

3. Show experienced users new areas of the product they might never have tried otherwise. This is great for increasing retention.

For ConnectHero, we could simply use a tooltip to provide some more context behind what's required for them to set up their account.

ConnectHero

Or, we could use a tooltip to show people around important areas of the product. A benefit of onboarding tooltips is that they're relatively easy to set up if you use a tool like Appcues, GainsightPX, WalkMe, or Pendo.

However, a lot of companies use onboarding tooltips incorrectly. Tell me if this sounds familiar? You log in to a product for the first time, then a tooltip pops up and tells you to click on a feature. Then, the tooltip prompts you to click on another feature. Once clicked, another tooltip offers to show you yet another feature until you've explored the entire product.

This is tooltip abuse. None of the activities leads the user toward experiencing meaningful value in the product. Remember Samuel Hullick's note: "People do not use software simply because they have tons of spare time and find clicking buttons enjoyable."

Key Takeaways:

1. Use onboarding tooltips to guide users toward experiencing meaningful value in the product.

2. People do not use software because they have tons of spare time and love to click buttons.

Onboarding tooltips can be a great way to show people what to do within a product. But what should you show people the first time they see your product's dashboard? Dummy data? That won't get anyone excited about a product. Nor does it help us get closer to experiencing value. If prospects had wanted to see dummy data, they would have signed up for a demo.

Instead of showing dummy data, explore empty states. They can guide users through the first few steps of setting up their account while being less intrusive than a product tour.

6. Empty States

Upon first login, most software applications are boring. There's no data specific to you; it's just the raw application. So what should you show people? An empty state can show people what they need to do to set up their account and experience meaningful value.

For ConnectHero, this could simply be showing people the steps they need to take to complete their account setup.

One of the benefits of empty states is that you immediately show users what needs to be done.

Gmail uses an empty state to help users set up and personalize their account:

Story Chief has an empty state to encourage users to craft their first story:

Buffer's empty state encourages you to connect your social media accounts. No one will use Buffer unless they complete this step. As such, Buffer ensures that people connect their social media accounts right away.

To decide what to include in an empty state, ask yourself:

- What steps does a user need to complete to experience a quick win?
- What is the most important step in my straight line?
- How can I make sure that the majority of users complete this step?

Key Takeaways:

1. Empty states are useful for when a user first lands on a product's dashboard.

2. Empty states should prompt users to take an action that will lead them closer to experiencing meaningful value in the product.

Do you have to use empty states, onboarding tooltips, checklists, and product tours? Absolutely not. Use product bumpers only when there's a need. The context in which you use each determines how effective it is.

Appendix III: Conversational Bumper

This is an excerpt of Chapter 13 from
Product-Led Growth by Wes Bush.

Conversational bumpers educate users, bring them back into the application, encourage them to upgrade their accounts, and notify users of new features. Whether you're using email, push notifications, explainer videos, direct mail, or even SMS, any communication medium can be a bumper.

Here's why you need conversational bumpers in your onboarding:

1. Educate users.
2. Set the right expectations.
3. Meet users where they are and pull them back into your app.
4. Increase motivation to use and buy your product.

One of the best ways to educate users and set the right expectations is through user onboarding emails; however, you can use the same content ideas for push notifications, direct mail, etc.

A main challenge with user onboarding emails is figuring out which emails you need to send. To simplify the process, I've compiled a list of the top nine user onboarding emails:

1. Welcome Emails

2. Usage Tips

3. Sales Touches

4. Case Study

5. Better-Life

6. Expiry Warning/Trial Extension

7. Customer Welcome Emails

8. Post-Trial Survey

The best user onboarding emails are an extension of your product. They have a magical ability to reach beyond your app or site to bring people back and move them toward customer happiness.

To get the most out of each section, draft a version of your user onboarding emails as we go through them. If you need to grab your pencil or laptop, I can wait.

1. Welcome Email

Welcome emails are triggered as soon as someone signs up for an account. One of the best parts about welcome emails is the high open rate. Aim for at least a 60% open rate.

Given that it's relatively easy to capture people's attention in a welcome email, what content should you put in it? It's tempting to write a lot about the product and ask the user to upgrade. I know you've got numbers to hit, but I encourage you not to take that approach.

Your welcome emails have two purposes. First, you need to train your audience to open your emails. Second, you need to set expectations for what's coming next.

With that in mind, make sure your welcome email has a clear call to action. If you recently launched your product, you can learn a lot by asking, "Why did you sign up to use our product?" Eventually, this will help you pinpoint the desired outcome that people have for your product.

If you're at a loss for words when drafting your welcome emails, don't worry. Here are two examples of welcome emails that follow the recommendations above:

Welcome Email 1:

Subject: *a personal hello*

Body:

Hey,

I'm one of the co-founders of [Your Company], and I'm excited you've decided to sign up.

The [Your Company] Team and I have poured our heart and soul into making [key outcome your product solves for] suck less, so I get really fired up when someone new, like you, joins the ranks.

My top priority is to make sure that you're able to [insert value proposition], so if you have any questions about our product, the website, or even my lackluster mustache, feel free to reply directly to this email.

I hope you can [accomplish key outcome in product]! Stay in touch!

P.S. Yes, I'm a real human.

– Wes, Co-Founder

Welcome Email 2

Subject: you're in — [company name]

Body:

Hey, thanks again for checking out [Your Company]. We help you:

- Customer benefit 1 ("You don't have to worry about X anymore.")
- Customer benefit 2 ("You can finally actually achieve Y, and in less time.")
- Customer benefit 3 ("It's free for the first month.")

But none of that's going to happen if you don't get started.

==> CREATE YOUR FIRST DASHBOARD HERE <== (your action-worded CTA)

Talk soon,

Wes

Key Takeaways:

- Welcome emails have the highest open rates of all user onboarding emails.
- Your welcome emails should train your audience to open your emails and set expectations for what's coming next.
- To make sure your audience receives this email (and that it doesn't get caught in a lovely spam filter), I recommend using plain text and no images, at least for the first email.

Welcome emails shouldn't be complicated. At some point, however, you have to get a bit more technical and offer a helping hand. That's when usage-tip emails come in handy.

2. Usage-Tip Emails

Usage-tip emails are helpful nudges that direct users to take steps in the product that set them up for success.

Be careful about what you encourage. For instance, if an activity you're encouraging doesn't help them experience meaningful value in the product, you dampen user motivation. Don't send emails that ask users to complete items that aren't part of your Straight-Line Onboarding track.

In general, usage-tip emails should do three things:

1. Direct users to a specific product page (e.g., "Manage Users" page).

2. Link to specific help-center articles or blog posts (e.g., "How to invite a user from outside your company").

3. Give actionable best practices or invite abandoned users to return.

If you can do these three things, you'll help more users succeed. Wistia's Soapbox product is a perfect example. After I created my first video, they sent a usage-tip email to encourage me to share it with someone.

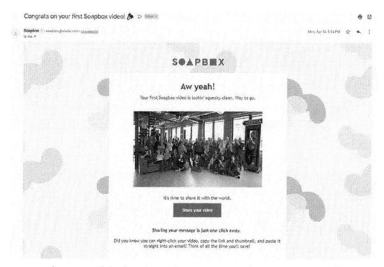

This email helped me learn more about Wistia's features but also made it easier to experience meaningful value by sharing the video.

Key Takeaways:

- Usage-tip emails nudge users to take steps in the product that set them up for success.
- The best usage tips are trigger-based and sent out once you do or don't complete an onboarding task.

If users miss a step in their Straight-Line Onboarding track, usage-tip emails can bump them toward the next step without being intrusive. Nevertheless, you'll eventually need to ask for the sale.

3.   Sales-Touch Emails

Sales-touch emails are exactly what the name implies. These emails can be automated, but the most important part is timing. If you send your sales-touch emails too soon, you'll turn people away. If you send them too late, you'll miss out on sales. The sweet spot for sending sales-touch emails is as soon as you deliver on your value, according to the UCD Model we covered in Part II.

For Databox, this is when you create and customize your first dashboard.

Subject: The hard part is over...

Body:

Hi Wesley,

You already did all the work to customize Databox, and the hard part is over...

Were you left with any questions? If so, let me know and I will answer them. Here are some common questions I get:

- *How to visualize goals and events from Google Analytics*

- *Can I build a dashboard with data stored in Google Sheets*
- *Is it possible to push custom data via API*
- *Do you offer a partner program for agencies*

Would love to learn more about you and what you are looking to accomplish with Databox. Just hit "reply" and let me know.

Thanks,

Andrew

Notice how the email doesn't come across as "salesy." The goal of the message is to help me get more value out of the platform. For your sales-touch emails, try two things:

1. Frame your sales-touch emails as a "success meeting" to celebrate the user achieving their desired outcome and to show them how to get more out of the product.

2. Invite inactive users to an orientation demo (e.g., "30-minute crash course on how to share documents and collaborate between teams").

You'll find that these "sales" emails are generally well-received. Users will be happy to hear what you have to say. If you're looking for a great template, Claire Suellentrop from Userlist.io shared a great email you can use:

Subject: *[Intriguing phrase about how a paid feature will make their lives easier.]*

Body:

Hi {{user.first_name | capitalize | default: "there"}},

[Pain point referenced in subject line] is no fun. [Describe a few problems the pain point causes, e.g., keeps them at the office late in the evening, forces them to delete important files or scatter them across multiple locations, wastes precious hours each week preparing for meetings and then having to reschedule.]

With [paid feature], you'll [get huge benefits, e.g., have the freedom to take Friday afternoons off, rest easy knowing their files are all in one place, increase productivity by 18%].

Since [paid feature] is part of our [paid plan name] plan, you'll just want to upgrade to [paid plan name], and you'll be good to go!

Just head to your billing page now, so you can start [getting benefit] [link].

Talk soon,

[Signature]

Key Takeaways:

- The sweet spot for sending sales-touch emails is as soon as someone experiences meaningful value in your product.
- Craft sales-touch emails to help users get more value out of the platform.

As you can see, sales-touch emails are largely about timing and offering a helping hand. However, sometimes we still need to clarify our product's value to build a convincing case to upgrade. One of the best ways to do that is through case-study emails.

4. Case-Study Emails

Whether you send a case-study email that includes a <u>video testimonial</u>, customer story, or old-fashioned case study, tell your customer's story about using the product. Invision does this by showcasing some of the incredible designs their customers have created with the product.

You're in good company

Tons of talented designers use InVision every day. Here's your chance to meet them.

Every Inside Design gives you a sneak peek at how design works at amazing companies. Discover how other designers work, get inspired, and build the amazing tools we use every day.

TAKE A SNEAK PEEK

How do you decide which testimonials to showcase? One of the best ways to decide is based on the objections you regularly receive when selling your product. These objections could be:

- The price is too high.
- We don't have the budget.
- It's not important right now.

Pair your top objection with a testimonial that addresses the objection head-on. For instance, if your top objection is that the price is too high, include a testimonial that showcases the amount of value the customer received from using your product. You address a top objection head-on, with your testimonial doing the heavy lifting.

If you send case-study emails before selling users on your product, you'll improve your free-to-paid conversion rate.

Key Takeaways:

- Use case-study emails to combat objections that users might have before they enter the buying phase.
- Make sure that each case-study email answers "What's in it for me?" for users.

Case studies are a powerful way to combat objections. However, sometimes we still need to communicate product benefits. One of the best ways to do this is through better-life emails.

5.   Better-Life Emails

Better-life emails communicate the benefits of the product. The main call to action in these emails is often to upgrade an account. But you can also direct people to try specific features.

Better-life emails don't tell a customer story. They focus on communicating the benefits of the product. Twist uses better-life emails to encourage people to "take back the workday" and sign up their team.

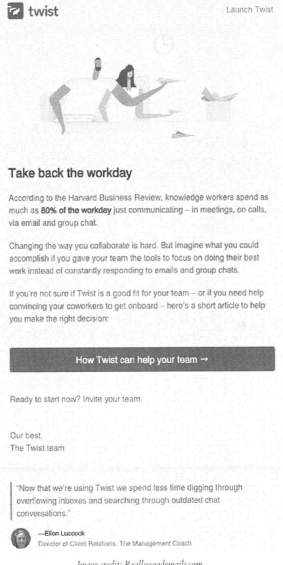

Image credit: Reallygoodemails.com

Showcase how your product improves a user's life. If you're selling a business intelligence tool, highlight how the user will no longer need to spend countless hours crunching numbers in Excel.

A common mistake with better-life emails is focusing only on the functional outcome of your product. Remember: You need to account for functional, social, and emotional outcomes. Here's a breakdown of each:

- Functional outcome. The core tasks that customers want to get done.
- Emotional outcome. How customers want to feel, or avoid feeling, as a result of the functional task.
- Social outcome. How customers want to be perceived by others.

If you know the three reasons why people buy your product, you can boost your conversion rate and ultimately acquire more customers. Before writing your better-life emails, ask yourself these questions:

- When talking to potential buyers, what benefits get them most excited?
- What benefits make it a no-brainer for people to upgrade?
  You'll have a better idea of which benefits to feature.

Key Takeaways:

- Better-life emails showcase the benefits of your product.
- The call to action can ask users to upgrade or help users experience product benefits for themselves.

Product-led companies often forget to emphasize the better life that their product offers during the trial period. By assuming users know the benefits, you miss an opportunity to restate your value and build a convincing case. If you have a free trial, that's a critical window: You have limited time to do so.

6. Expiry-Warning Emails

Expiry-warning emails remind the user to upgrade before a free trial ends. Freemium models don't use expiry-warning emails because part of the product is free forever. That said, if you have a hybrid model (with a free trial and freemium offer), expiry emails can still motivate users to upgrade.

If you have an opt-out free trial (you require a credit card upfront), you must send expiry-warning emails. If you don't, you're guaranteed to annoy users and flood your support reps with refund demands. Think about it: What did you do the last time you signed up for a product with a credit card and missed the deadline? Did you continue paying for the product for a month or two before realizing you forgot to cancel? Or did you demand support to give you a refund because you forgot to cancel your plan?

I won't dive into whether you should or shouldn't have a credit card requirement during the free-trial sign-up, but, as a general rule, make it easy for users to cancel their account. Squarespace sends emails to notify users that their trial will expire soon. This email is great because it restates the value proposition and why it makes sense to upgrade now.

Your free trial expires in 24 hours.

Your 14-day trial for **http://amy-smith-podj.squarespace.com** ends in 24 hours and we hope you've enjoyed the experience. Our plans start at $8 per month and by **upgrading now**, you'll ensure your website stays live and can take full advantage of these great features:

| CLOUD HOSTING | SITE ANALYTICS | FREE DOMAIN | 24/7 SUPPORT |

Have questions about upgrading?

Our support team can answer any question about upgrading to a full Squarespace account. We're on call 24 hours a day, 7 days a week, and respond to all questions in under an hour. If you need assistance, contact us anytime by visiting our **Help Center**.

UPGRADE NOW

Let us know if there's anything we can do.

Expiry-warning emails have three goals:

1.   Set clear expectations.

Trials end—that's just how they work. However, if users provide a credit card as part of the sign-up process, they'll be charged automatically. Make sure to give them a few days' notice about the charge so they aren't surprised.

The last thing you want to do is annoy users who forgot that they signed up for your product and paid accidentally.

When they figure out that they were charged, they'll demand a refund.

Even if you don't require a credit card, you want to craft a painless transition to paying customers.

The best way to do that is by:

- Giving users as much notice as possible.
- Making it crystal clear when the trial expires and what happens if the trial expires.
- Providing a call to action for users to upgrade.

2. Make it easy for users to upgrade, cancel, or do nothing.

Some people will upgrade, and some won't. As such, you want it to be easy for people to upgrade. Still, most people won't upgrade, so it should be easy for users to cancel their accounts. The expiry email can make this process easy and leave a positive impression.

3. Communicate how users can get help.

The transition from trial to paying customer can be stressful. Once a customer decides to use your software, they want to make the transition seamless. When will they be charged? How can they get approval from their team? In some cases, they may also wonder if they can maintain data from their current trial.

There are countless questions and concerns. Make sure that customers know that they can get help and know where to find it. Even if you check the box on all of the recommended ways of using expiry emails, you need to avoid some common mistakes.

Common mistakes with expiry-warning emails

Trial expiration emails serve two very different user types:

1. People who want to become paying customers.
2. People who don't.

In the same email, you need to address the needs of both groups—without making the email confusing. Most mistakes in expiry-warning emails stem from these conflicting goals.

1. Failing to provide enough advanced notice

Weekends, vacations, and travel can interfere with the timing of a trial expiration. It's important to give people a heads up. That way, users know exactly when a trial will expire, whether they want to transition to a paying customer (and avoid a service interruption), or if they want to cancel their account (and avoid an unintentional payment).

I recommend sending an expiry-warning email at least three days before the end of each user's trial. This gives users enough time to make a decision to move forward with your product or not.

2. Assuming that the recipient wants to begin paying for the product

One of the biggest mistakes I see companies make with expiry-warning emails is not including the product's main value proposition. Offering a compelling reason to take action results in (surprise) more people taking action.

Just because someone signs up for a free trial doesn't mean that they're ready to buy. Most people who sign up for your free trial or freemium model won't convert. You need to include compelling reasons for someone to upgrade. Screenhero proves this point by failing to include a convincing reason to upgrade.

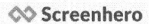

Hi Matthew,

Thanks for signing up for Screenhero. We hope you have been enjoying your free trial.

Unfortunately, your free trial is ending in 3 days.

We'd love to keep you as a customer, and there is still time to complete your subscription! Simply visit your account dashboard to subscribe.

As a reminder, when your trial expires you will be automatically placed on the free guest plan.

If you have any questions or feedback, just reply to this email, and we'll get right back to you.

-- The Screenhero Team

On the other hand, Squarespace's expiry email does a great job highlighting the key benefits of the platform. Now we know why we should upgrade, right?

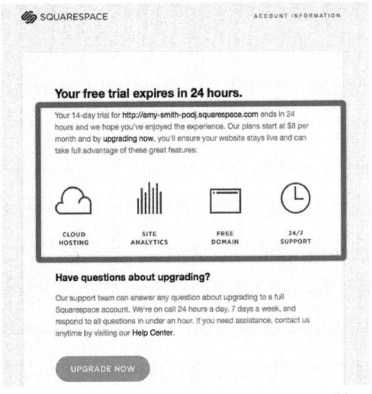

To recap, your expiry-warning emails should be able to answer these questions:

1. Why should I upgrade?
2. How do I upgrade?
3. How much time do I have left?
4. What happens when the trial is over?
5. How do I cancel? (if you require a credit card.)
6. Where can I go if I need help?

Key Takeaways:

- You must send expiry emails if you have an opt-out free trial. If you don't, users will forget they signed up and get mad when they get charged for a product they haven't been using.

- Restate your value proposition in each expiry email to create a compelling reason for users to upgrade.
- Make it incredibly easy for someone to upgrade in the expiry email.

If you have a free trial, expiry emails are a great way to motivate users to upgrade—there's genuine urgency behind the email. However, what do you do when people take you up on your offer? For starters, send a customer-welcome email.

7. Customer-Welcome Emails

Have you ever purchased a plane ticket on a questionable travel website, then waited nervously for email confirmation? When you buy something from a brand you don't trust, waiting for a confirmation email can feel like an eternity. Your new customers feel the same way.

To reduce that anxiety, use customer-welcome emails:

1. Reassure users that they made the right decision.
2. Remind users of what they can do with the platform.
3. Set expectations for what comes next (e.g., will a customer success rep reach out?).

Too many businesses don't welcome new customers immediately. Most reach out manually, but it takes time. In the interim, new customers become nervous, wondering if they made the right decision. Don't make your new customer think twice. Remind them why they made the right decision. Spotify welcomes users as soon as they upgrade to premium:

Image credit to reallygoodemails.com

One thing Spotify has done really well is to remind users why they upgraded, showcasing the value of the platform. This email increases user motivation to check out the product and listen to some great music without ads. If you have a freemium product, recap your premium features so that users can explore them right away.

Key Takeaways:

- Customer-welcome emails must be sent as soon as users upgrade.
- The point of customer-welcome emails is to reassure users that they made the right decision, remind them what they can now do with the platform, and set expectations for what comes next.

Customer-welcome emails are a great way to remind new customers that they made the right choice. But no matter how hard you try, not everyone will convert—nor should they. Your product might not be the right fit. It might be too expensive. The list goes on.

To improve your free-trial experience, you need to learn why it didn't work out for some users.

This is why I almost always recommend using post-trial survey emails.

8. Post-Trial Survey Emails

Even with the most amazing free-trial experience, most users won't convert. Some aren't a good fit. Some might not have had time to check out your tool. Others, well, they might have needed more time or someone to help them learn to use the product.

There are countless reasons, but you'll never learn to understand them if you don't implement post-trial survey emails. For Autopilot, their post-trial survey email looks like this:

Subject: *Wesley, have 60 seconds to share why?*

Body:

Hi Wesley,

I noticed that you have not purchased Autopilot so far. I'd love to hear your thoughts on your trial experience in this super quick survey. It will only take 60 seconds (we have measured it!)

Your response will help us focus on improving your trial experience and better meet your needs.

Thanks in advance,

Lauren

What I like about this email is how it gets straight to the point and encourages you to fill out a quick survey:

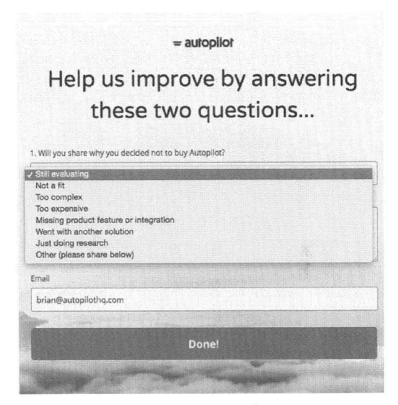

Based on your response, <u>Autopilot</u> enrolls you in an automated sequence. Autopilot recommends starting with this list:

- Still evaluating → Offer a trial extension.
- Not a fit → Drop into nurture.
- Too complex → Schedule a customer success call.
- Too expensive → Provide a one-time discount.
- Went with another solution → Send top-of-funnel lead-nurturing emails to stay top-of-mind if the other service doesn't work out.
- Just doing research → Add to nurture (notice the nurturing trend?).

- Missing product feature or integration → See if it's on your product roadmap; if so, let them know when it's live.

If you use your free-trial survey in this manner, you'll combat buyer objections and provide a more personalized experience for each user.

Key Takeaways:

- Post-trial survey emails can improve your free-to-paid conversion rate if you trigger certain events based on user feedback. For instance, if a user says the product was too complex, you can have a customer success representative reach out to walk them through the product.

As in bowling, if you don't get a strike in the first throw, you have another shot. So, why not use post-trial survey emails as a way to rekindle the opportunity and provide an incredible experience? After all, these same users were interested in using your product for a specific reason. Let's help them out.

Endnotes

1.   Producer, Dee Reddy Podcast, et al. "Onboarding Customers for Long-Term Success [Complete Guide]." Inside Intercom, 30 July 2020, www.intercom.com/blog/onboarding-guide/.

2.   Fishkin, Rand. "Lost and Founder : a Painfully Honest Field Guide to the Startup World." Lost and Founder, Portfolio/Penguin, 26 Feb. 2018, www.nima.today/wp-content/uploads/2018/11/Lost-And-Founder-Rand-Fishkin.pdf. Page 166

3.   McClure, Dave. "Product Marketing for Pirates: AARRR! (Aka Startup Metrics for Internet Marketing & Product Management)." Master of 500 Hats, 20 June 2007, 500hats.typepad.com/500blogs/2007/06/internet-market.html.

4.   Kim, Jonathan. "The Power of Intentional Onboarding for Product-Led Companies." OpenView, 7 June 2019, openviewpartners.com/blog/the-power-of-intentional-onboarding-for-product-led-companies/.

5.   "From 0 to $1B - Slack's Founder Shares Their Epic Launch Strategy." First Round Review, firstround.com/review/From-0-to-1B-Slacks-Founder-Shares-Their-Epic-Launch-Strategy/.

6.   Reichheld, Fred. "Prescription for Cutting Costs." Prescription for Cutting Costs, BAIN & COMPANY, INC, media.bain.com/Images/BB_Prescription_cutting_costs.pdf.

7. "Never Mix Up Features with Benefits Ever Again: UserOnboard: User Onboarding." UserOnboard, www.useronboard.com/features-vs-benefits/.

8. "Guides Archive." *Center on the Developing Child at Harvard University*, developingchild.harvard.edu/guide/.

9. Wolchonok, Dan. *Retention Experiments.* cdn2.hubspot.net/hubfs/120299/SaaSFest_Presentations/SaaSFestPres o-Dan-RetentionIsKing.pdf.

10. Murariu, Claudiu. "4 Essential Questions for Optimizing Retention." Product Analytics Software for Product Leaders, www.innertrends.com/blog/4-essential-questions-for-optimizing-retention.

11. Skok, David. "Top Two Reasons for Churn." For Entrepreneurs, 3 Jan. 2018, www.forentrepreneurs.com/top-two-reasons-for-churn/.

12. Desai, Neel. "Solid Customer Onboarding Drives Higher Retention, Willingness to Pay." Subscription Business Financial Metrics. Absolutely Free., 20 Feb. 2019, www.profitwell.com/recur/all/positive-onboarding-boosts-retention-wtp.

13. Winters, Casey. "Why Onboarding Is the Most Crucial Part of Your Growth Strategy." Medium, Greylock Perspectives, 27 June 2017, news.greylock.com/why-onboarding-is-the-most-crucial-part-of-your-growth-strategy-8f9ad3ec8d5e.

14. Bush, Wes. "The First 7 Minutes of Onboarding." *ProductLed*, 22 Feb. 2021, productled.com/the-first-7-minutes-of-onboarding/.

15. Taylor, Marcus. "58 Form Design Best Practices & Form UX Examples." Venture Harbour, 22 Sept. 2020, www.ventureharbour.com/form-design-best-practices/.

16. Bonnie, Emily. "The Mobile Marketer's Guide to Mastering User Retention." *CleverTap*, 19 Aug. 2020, clevertap.com/blog/guide-to-user-retention/.

17. Cox, Jeff. "The Ultimate Guide to Freemium." HubSpot Blog, 4 May 2020, blog.hubspot.com/service/freemium.

18. Tunguz, Tomasz. "Top 10 Learnings from the Redpoint Free Trial Survey by @Ttunguz." Tomasz Tunguz, 6 Feb. 2019, tomtunguz.com/top-10-learnings-from-the-redpoint-free-trial-survey/.

19. Kim, Jonathan. "The Power of Intentional Onboarding for Product-Led Companies." OpenView, 7 June 2019, openviewpartners.com/blog/the-power-of-intentional-onboarding-for-product-led-companies/.

20. Belsky, Scott. "The First 15 Seconds." Medium, Positive Slope, 2 Feb. 2016, medium.com/positiveslope/the-first-15-seconds-9590d7dabc.

21. "Maslow's Hierarchy of Needs." Wikipedia, Wikimedia Foundation, 16 May 2021, en.wikipedia.org/wiki/Maslow%27s_hierarchy_of_needs.

22. Telegraph, The. "Panel of Doctors Agrees: A Real-Life James Bond Would Have Been Dead within First Seven Minutes of Skyfall." Nationalpost, National Post, 9 Apr. 2015, nationalpost.com/entertainment/panel-of-doctors-agrees-a-real-life-james-bond-would-have-been-dead-within-first-seven-minutes-of-skyfall.

23. Carolyn Dewar, Scott Keller, Johanne Lavoie, and Leigh M. Weiss, McKinsey & Company, Organization Practice, "How Do I Drive Effective Collaboration to Deliver Real Business Impact?" September 2009.

24. Belsky, Scott. The First 15 Seconds, 13 Nov. 2013, www.managementexchange.com/blog/true-collaboration-embraces-conflict.

25. Producer, Dee Reddy Podcast, et al. "Onboarding Customers for Long-Term Success [Complete Guide]." Inside Intercom, 30 July 2020, blog.intercom.com/designing-first-run-experiences-to-delight-users/.

26. Kathy. "Creating Passionate Users." Creating Passionate Users: Upgrade Your Users, Not Just Your Product, 2 Feb. 2005, headrush.typepad.com/creating_passionate_users/2005/02/upgrade_ your_us.html.

27. Christensen, Clayton M., et al. "What Customers Want from Your Products." *HBS Working Knowledge*, 16 Jan. 2006, hbswk.hbs.edu/item/5170.html.

28. Klement, Alan. "When Coffee and Kale Compete."

29. "Maslow's Hierarchy of Needs." Wikipedia, Wikimedia Foundation, 16 May 2021, en.wikipedia.org/wiki/Maslow%27s_hierarchy_of_needs.

30. State of Marketing Strategy Report 2018, State of Marketing Strategy Report 2018.

31. State of Marketing Strategy Report 2018, State of Marketing Strategy Report 2018.

32. Murphy, Lincoln. "SaaS Free Trial Conversion Rate Benchmarks." Customer-Centric Growth by Lincoln Murphy, sixteenventures.com/saas-free-trial-benchmarks.

33. Tunguz, Tomasz. "Top 10 Learnings from the Redpoint Free Trial Survey by @Ttunguz." Tomasz Tunguz, 6 Feb. 2019, tomtunguz.com/top-10-learnings-from-the-redpoint-free-trial-survey/.

34. Palihapitiya, Chamath. How We Put Facebook on the Path to 1 Billion Users. genius.com/Chamath-palihapitiya-how-we-put-facebook-on-the-path-to-1-billion-users-annotated.

35. Ellis, Sean. Putting It All Together – How Josh Elman Identified A Growth Driver At Twitter. 25 Apr. 2017, mattermark.com/putting-it-all-together-how-josh-elman-identified-a-growth-driver-at-twitter/.

36. Palihapitiya , Chamath. Chamath Palihapitiya - How We Put Facebook on the Path to 1 Billion Users. 10 Jan. 2013, www.youtube.com/watch?v=raIUQP71SBU&feature=youtu.b e&t=21m5s.

37. Cook, David. How Do You Find Insights like Facebook's "7 Friends in 10 Days" to Grow Your Product Faster? 15 Mar. 2013, www.quora.com/How-do-you-find-insights-like-Facebooks-7-friends-in-10-days-to-grow-your-product-faster/answer/David-Cook-6.

38. Berman, Jillian, "The IKEA Effect: Study Finds Consumers Over-Value Products They Build Themselves", September 2011

39. "Basic Onboarding." Userlist, userlist.com/docs/campaign-templates/onboarding/.

40. "Using Progress Bars in Online Forms." Zuko Form Analytics, www.zuko.io/blog/progress-bars-in-online-forms.

41. Peet, Whitney Rudeseal. 18 Apr. 2019, twitter.com/whitneyrpeet/status/1118594327691788288.

42. Mullin, Shanelle. "Social Proof: What It Is, Why It Works, and How to Use It." May 2021, https://cxl.com/blog/is-social-proof-really-that-important/

43. 40 INSANE EMAIL MARKETING STATS PROVE IT'S THRIVING. robbenmedia.com/email-marketing-stats/.

44. Skillman, Peter. "The Design Challenge (Also Called Spaghetti Tower):" Medium, Medium, 14 Apr. 2019, medium.com/@peterskillman/the-design-challenge-also-called-spaghetti-tower-cda62685e15b.

45. Balfour, Brian. [500DISTRO] The Scientific Method: How to Design & Track Viral Growth Experiments. 6 Aug. 2014, www.slideshare.net/500startups/02-brian-balfour-hub-spot-final.

46. Hart, Dani. "Learn Faster with a Growth Process." Medium, Growth Hackers, 22 Sept. 2017, blog.growthhackers.com/learn-faster-with-a-growth-process-85f6affde4af.

47. Mullin, By: Shanelle, et al. "The Growth Marketing Process: Stop Looking For The Magic Pill." CXL, 8 Sept. 2020, cxl.com/blog/growth-marketing-process/.

48. Tunguz, Tomasz. "Top 10 Learnings from the Redpoint Free Trial Survey by @Ttunguz." Tomasz Tunguz, 6 Feb. 2019, tomtunguz.com/top-10-learnings-from-the-redpoint-free-trial-survey/.

49. "SLACK TECHNOLOGIES, INC. Shares of Class A Common Stock." Document, 26 Apr. 2019, www.sec.gov/Archives/edgar/data/1764925/000162828019004786/s lacks-1.htm.

50. Janz, Christoph. Five Ways to Build a $100 Million Business. 5 Oct. 2014, christophjanz.blogspot.com/2014/10/five-ways-to-build-100-million-business.html.

51. Efti, Steli. "How to create your ideal customer profile for B2B lead generation." Close.com Blog, https://blog.close.com/ideal-customer-profile/

52. Skaletsky, Derek. "The 'All My Shit's in There' (AMSIT) Factor — a SaaS Product Theory." Derek Skaletsky, 1 July 2020, dskaletsky.medium.com/.

53. Sacks, David. "Freemium vs Free Trial: Which Is Better for SaaS Startups?" Medium, Craft Ventures, 9 Dec. 2019, medium.com/craft-ventures/freemium-vs-free-trial-which-is-better-for-saas-startups-97b9ac737597.

Made in the USA
Columbia, SC
19 September 2022